RESTORING TEXAS

Raiford Stripling at his drawing board, San Augustine. (Photograph by Dixon Daniel)

RESTORING TEXAS

*Raiford Stripling's Life
and Architecture*

By

MICHAEL McCULLAR

Foreword by

FRANK D. WELCH

TEXAS A&M UNIVERSITY PRESS

COLLEGE STATION

Library of Congress Cataloging-in-Publication Data

McCullar, Michael, 1951–
    Restoring Texas.

    Bibliography: p.
    Includes index.
    1. Stripling, Raiford Leak, 1910–
2. Architects—Texas—Biography. 3. Historic
buildings—Texas—Conservation and restoration.
I. Title.
NA737.S73M35   1985   720'. 92'4 [B]   85-40052
ISBN 0-89096-254-5

Manufactured in the United States of America
FIRST EDITION

To Fred Wulff

Contents

Illustrations

COLOR PLATES
following p. 98

Foreword

I**T** wasn't so long ago that Victorian cottages weren't restored to house lawyers' offices or that a major bank didn't feel compelled to incorporate the remnant facade of an ornate movie theater into its new high rise. It is also easily within memory that the notion of an old building being important, for reasons deeper than just utility or ornament, was widely considered to be little more than a stubborn, romantic eccentricity. But as a state and a nation we are currently in the thrall of our architectural past. It's a situation long overdue, and if obsessive at times, it may be the catch-up price we pay for having allowed thousands of valuable buildings of all sizes and styles to be razed over the years. Preservationists have an easy time of it now, but it was only fairly recently (1966) that, with major public effort, they could not prevent the destruction of Pennsylvania Station, one of New York's and the nation's great monuments.

It is timely that Michael McCullar has written the story of an architect who has practiced historic preservation in Deep East Texas for some forty years with an enduring and independent judgment about what is "correct," and without a great deal of notice. It's a wonderful story, and timely because of the upcoming Texas sesquicentennial, which causes us to reflect upon the state's history and to appreciate those indige-

nous Texans who have put integrity and color into it. Raiford has spent most of his career quietly preserving some of the most visible aspects of that history while affecting his region—one of the state's most historic—as much as any man.

This book about Raiford Stripling of San Augustine, Texas, is a biography of a place as well as a man. It's impossible to separate Raiford from his special roots in time and Texas. Deep East Texas is a unique part of the state, the edge of a culture that flowed west out of the Deep South in the nineteenth century. When the settlers, traveling from Mississippi and beyond, crossed the Sabine River into the region we call East Texas and saw the streams, forests, and iron-red earth, they sank stakes into a land that looked like home, extending the limits of the Old South.

At the western extremity of Southern culture when it was settled, and being situated on the Camino Real, San Augustine was an important link between the Southwest and the South and—more important to us today—was a vital reflection of the Greek Revival architecture of the Old Confederacy. Raiford's time as a youngster was idyllically Southern, blessed with a closeness to the earth and to adults to whom local and regional history were living subjects. His entry into the profession after his graduation from college was marked by the devastation of the Great Depression and its discouraging effects on the expectations of the young. An irony is that from that national breakdown emerged a federal program for documenting the country's historic buildings. It was the beginning of a validation of our young but rich architectural heritage that eventually evolved into the current widespread commitment for the preservation of our constructed past.

After graduating from Texas A&M in 1931, Raiford apprenticed while working for various public agencies at state and national levels as the depression and World War II consumed the nation's energy. In 1947 he returned to his native San Augustine to practice a special architecture.

Raiford's reputation as a sensitive, scholarly, and headstrong restoration architect grew constantly and surely after his work on Mission Espíritu Santo in Goliad for the National Park Service in the 1930s. In his subsequent work on the early nineteenth-century architecture of San Augustine are

perhaps the best examples of a practice that has taken him all over the state. He has put a light on these utterly simple—and spiritually Modern—buildings, restoring them in a manner as honorable as the houses themselves, which are free of artifice and cant, and full of restraint and dignity. In elegant repose, they appear as they might have shortly after their construction, with none of the gussied-up look that many restored buildings have. No embalmer's art here. They are as direct and self-effacing as Raiford Stripling the man, inspiring us as they remind us of the strength and economy of Greek Revival design.

After a visit to San Augustine not long ago to meet Raiford and see the historic architecture there, I returned to Dallas with a certain sense of renewal. The trip over had been full of anticipation, the trip back full of reward. Being with Raiford and seeing those houses had made me glad to be an architect.

Frank D. Welch

Acknowledgments

THIS book is the outgrowth of a symposium held September 10, 1983, at the Institute of Texan Cultures in San Antonio to honor Raiford Stripling and his work. The chief organizer of the symposium was Gordon Echols, a professor of urban and regional planning at Texas A&M—co-sponsor of the event—who allowed me free access to all correspondence, grant applications, and videotapes relating to the symposium; let me use his office from time to time; read the first draft of the manuscript; and without whose agreeable assistance this book would have been considerably more difficult to write.

I would also like to extend special thanks to Ford Albritton, Jr., for commissioning it; H. Davis Mayfield III, for recommending me as its author; the late Fred Wulff, for giving me the tools to write it in a year's time; Victor Treat, for suggesting that such a book be written; David Woodcock, for his enthusiastic support and good judgment; Raiford Stripling, for letting me stay in the Garrett House during my first visit to San Augustine and for being so patient and indulgent throughout the year; Raggy Stripling, Robert Stripling, Frances Hartley, Roberta Garner, C. A. Johnson, Pete Mathews, Jesse Leo Norton, and Bradley Vosper, for their special insights; Mary Jane Stripling, for her wonderful jalapeño hamburgers; Katy Capt Whisenant, for laying such a firm groundwork with her master's thesis monograph on Raiford; Griff Smith and Dixon Daniel, for their skills with a camera; Larry Paul Fuller, for lining up the perfect workplace and for providing some expert editorial assistance; Saundra Wark, for her expert administrative and technical assistance; Frank Welch, for his wise and eloquent input; Nancy Fuller, for being such good company; Kay McCullar, for somehow teaching me to appreciate the written word; Katherine Wulff, for sustaining me; and David McCullar, who spent an inordinate amount of time with his father in the first year of his life but who I trust will turn out all right in spite of it.

I would also like to express my gratitude to the authors of two excellent histories from which I drew a good deal of information about Texas A&M University and the historic preservation movement in the United States: Henry C. Dethloff, *A Centennial History of Texas A&M University, 1876–1976* (Texas A&M University Press, 1975); and Charles B. Hosmer, Jr., *Preservation Comes of Age: From Williamsburg to the National Trust, 1926–1949* (University Press of Virginia, 1981).

This project would also have been considerably more difficult without the help of the following individuals, who did much—either directly or indirectly—to facilitate my research and writing: Leon Adickes, Lin Altman, Lavonia Jenkins Barnes, David Chapman, Laura Cicarella, Bartlett Cocke, Dennis Cordes, Phil Creer, José Miguel Fernandez, Lavonne Garland, Eugene George, Paul Glenn, Maj. Michael Hardin, David and Binnie Hoffman, Larry Hollis, John Huntsinger, Inez Lasell, John Lash, Amy Freeman Lee, Peter Maxon, Mark Meyer, J. D. Miller, Peter and Rawsie Payne, Boone Powell, John Riley, Dick Rizzo, Charles Sappington, Judy Schiebel, Bonnie Sears, Andy Sieverman, Hank Smith, Lila Stillson, Kathleen Todd, Vincent Transano, Amy A. Troyansky, and Mrs. Gene Waugh.

My work was also greatly aided by the staffs of the Austin History Center; Barker Texas History Center at the University of Texas at Austin; Battle Hall Library at the University of Texas at Austin; Chicago Historical Society; Custom Photographic Labs in Austin; Galveston Historical Foundation; Historic Waco Foundation; Office of the Registrar at Pratt Institute in Brooklyn, New York; Office of the Registrar at Southwestern University in Georgetown, Texas; San Antonio Conservation Society; Texas A&M University Archives; Texas Board of Architectural Examiners; and Texas Historical Commission.

RESTORING   TEXAS

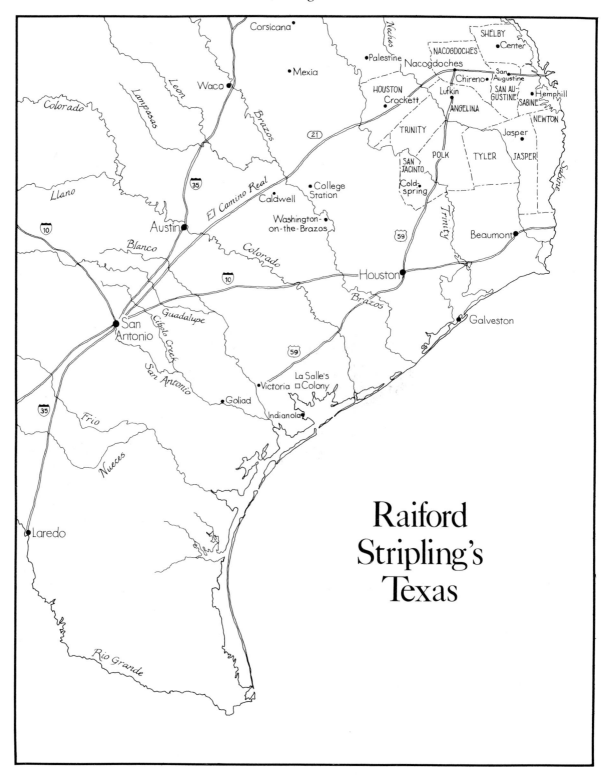

Raiford
Stripling's
Texas

CHAPTER 1

Introduction: A Man and His Place

East from Lufkin, Texas State Highway 103 pierces the northern tip of the Angelina National Forest like a rifle shot. It is a direct, no-nonsense kind of route, rolling some with the contour of the land but swaying little from its course. Before entering the forest, the two-lane highway crosses over a portion of the Sam Rayburn Reservoir, a 114,300-acre lake formed in the mid-1960s by the damming of the Angelina River. Where 103 first crosses the water, the dead gray tops of hardwood trees that once shaded the slopes of the river valley stick grotesquely above the water like some kind of skeletal remains. Farther on, inside the forest, 103 is enveloped by pine trees, thick stands of loblolly and shortleaf planted in rows and growing to the shoulders of the roadway.

North toward San Augustine, Highway 147 leaves the national forest and enters upon rolling green pastureland trimmed in hardwood and pine. Here there is more of a variety of vegetation; oak, ash, gum, and hickory have matured handsomely since the virgin longleaf was logged out, most of it gone by the turn of the century. Hardwood has actually mingled with the pine in this part of East Texas as long as the white man has, which is what drew him here in the first place. Areas of pure pine or dense underbrush, as in the national forest and Big Thicket to the south, or the denuded blackland prairie and arid plains farther west, offered little enticement to settlers who judged the value of land by the vegetation already on it.

In terms of its people as well as its trees, this part of the state is not what most people think of when they think of Texas. The legendary cowboy culture of the state, played out against a backdrop of wide-open spaces and prickly-pear cactus, does not reach this far east. Deep East Texas is more like western Louisiana—or like portions of Alabama, Georgia, and Mississippi, states of the lower South whence many of its settlers came, stopping here because the surroundings reminded them of home. Unlike the enterprising grain and cotton farmers from Tennessee, Kentucky, and Missouri who populated North Texas, those who settled the piney woods were largely subsistence farmers. By 1860, the typical East Texan lived in a log house, farmed a few acres of corn and cotton, and shied away from the clamor of the marketplace and the building of cities.

In recent years, as Texas has gained some worldwide renown as a dynamically urban state, the differences between Deep East Texas and the rest of the state have become even greater. Houston booming to the south in the late 1970s indeed affected the piney woods and its inhabitants, but mainly by retirees and weekend pleasure seekers swooping onto the lakes for fishing and waterskiing. The most apparent effect of Houston's prosperity is manifested here in lavish weekend retreats and retirement homes overlooking the recreational reservoirs. Alongside this prosperity almost 25 percent of the residents of San Augustine County, for example—one-third of whom are black—exist below the poverty level.[1] And although such regional metropolises as Lufkin, Tyler, Longview, and Nacogdoches have thrived as much as Houston has, the East Texas outback just beyond their city limits is just about as rural and as rustic as it ever was.

Reflecting the earth and vegetation of the region, small frame houses and weathered barns (along with the ubiquitous mobile home, the "new log cabin") lie hidden in the shadows along the roadway. On toward San Augustine, the sandy soil turns red, showing up first in the logging roads, then in the driveways and stone chimneys closer to town, finally in the red-brick buildings that surround the courthouse square.

Like its region, San Augustine, fifteen miles west of the Sabine in the heart of the East Texas Redlands, is a vestige of the Old South, an antebellum town that evokes the character and texture of a different age—or of different ages. It was the site of a Spanish mission in the early 1700s, Nuestra Señora de los Dolores de los Ais (Our Lady of Sorrows of the Ais [Indians]). Then in the early 1800s, strategically situated as it was on El Camino Real (the King's Highway), it functioned as an inland gateway for the settlement of Texas, along with the coastal ports of Galveston and Indianola. Settled in 1833, San Augustine became a kind of Texan Saint Louis, serving as a last outpost of civilization for migratory Americans and, in some ways, as the first sign of civilization for those who had just run the harrowing gauntlet of No-Man's-Land. For years, this lawless, twenty-five-mile stretch of King's Highway between Natchitoches, Louisiana, and the Sabine was claimed by the Spanish, French, Americans, and Indians as territorial boundaries shifted. It was also a haven for bandits and slave traders and was filled, as one account has it, "with love, hate, jealousy, generosity, selfishness, prosperity and despair."[2]

The King's Highway as a whole (also known as the Royal Road, the Contraband Trail, the Old Natchez–San Antonio Trace, and, most recently, Louisiana and Texas State Highways 6 and 21) began as a buffalo path and eventually became part of the Caddo Indian trail system. In time, as colonists set out from Mexico City to claim these northern lands for Spain, the route stretched from Natchitoches all the way to Mexico City, where the Spanish viceroy (the king's representative) resided and where, as royal tradition dictated, all official roads had to lead. The first town astride this important route west of the Sabine, San Augustine came to be called "The Cradle of Texas" during the Texas War for Independence, for it was said that any man—whether French, Spanish, or American—entering the town instantly became a Texan.

San Augustine is also said to have been the first town in Texas laid out in the "American plan," which revolved around a central courthouse square, rather than in the "Spanish plan," which specified that the central square be left open as a plaza and designated specific sites around it for churches

---

[1]U.S. Department of Commerce, Bureau of the Census, *1980 Census of Population*, vol. I, *Characteristics of the Population, Chapter C, General Social and Economic Characteristics, Part 45, Texas* (Washington, D.C., July, 1983), pp. 45–54.

[2]Louis R. Nardini, *No Man's Land: A History of El Camino Real* (New Orleans: Pelican Publishing, 1961), p. x.

and municipal buildings.[3] San Augustine University was chartered in 1837, the same year the town was incorporated, and during the days of the Republic, when cotton became king, San Augustine prospered as a regional center of commerce and culture. Its early citizens included two governors of Texas, James Pinckney Henderson (the state's first governor, whose statue commands the front of the courthouse), and O. M. Roberts, who served as governor from 1879 to 1883. (Prominent citizens in later years included lieutenant governors John Greer, 1845–53, and Ben Ramsey, 1951–61, as well as U.S. Ambassador Edward Clark, chief envoy to Australia from 1965 to 1968.) However, after the so-called Regulator-Moderator War of 1839–44, a local feud that disrupted the town's all-important trade with Louisiana markets, San Augustine's vitality began to slip. Population declined throughout the late 1800s, and in 1890 a devastating fire that leveled much of the downtown area seemed to seal San Augustine's fate. By the turn of the century, the population numbered 261, down from 920 in 1870. And although population has steadily increased ever since, at an average rate of about 1.2 percent per year (to around 3,000 in 1984), the city has never regained its antebellum health or stature. Once one of the most dynamic settlements in the state, twentieth-century San Augustine has become just another stunted East Texas town.

One effect of all this, of course, is the pristine preservation of architecture often found in towns that have not been particularly prosperous. There is a certain irony in the fact that, while a boom in the early nineteenth century created the rich architectural fabric of San Augustine, there was no subsequent boom to destroy it. Economi-

cally stagnant for the last century, more or less, San Augustine and its environs feature a wealth of historic buildings; at every turn official state medallions mark houses, churches, and schools representing a full range of nineteenth-century styles, from hand-hewn log to Victorian—preserved as if in amber.

The finest of this architecture was built in San Augustine in large part because of the energy and expertise of one Augustus Phelps, a carpenter by trade who, at the age of twenty-four, came to San Augustine from Philadelphia in 1838 to design and build some of the earliest Greek Revival houses in Texas. Others contributed to the boom, of course, but Phelps did more to set standards for stylistic and material excellence than anybody else. And Phelps was fortunate. Not only would the stagnant economy of San Augustine protect his handiwork for the next hundred years or so, but there would also be born here a native son who would be reared among the historic structures of the town, who would become well versed in their histories, and who would eventually devote his professional life to immortalizing the kind of architecture (among others) that Phelps created.

This native son is San Augustine architect Raiford Leak Stripling, going strong in his mid-seventies as a partner with his son Raggy in one of only a handful of architectural practices in eleven Deep East Texas counties (the twelfth county of the region, nearby Angelina, with Lufkin as its county seat, lists thirteen registered architects—more than all the other counties combined). Raiford has been a specialist in historic preservation since the 1930s—long before it became a fashionable tax break—out of a sheer love for old buildings, particularly those that tell of Texas history. He also happens to be, in the words of San Antonio poet and author Amy Freeman Lee, one

[3]George Louis Crocket, *Two Centuries in East Texas: A History of San Augustine County and Surrounding Territory from 1685* (San Augustine: Christ Episcopal Church, 1932), p. 105.

of those unmistakably "true Texans" like Dobie, Webb, Bedichek, and perhaps O'Neil Ford—"what the British call a glorious eccentric"—who is as much a product of his region as is the object of his livelihood, in spite of the fact that his region may not seem as typically "Texan" as other parts of the state. So undeniably of his place, Raiford was not—until a few years ago—very well known outside of it; his almost forty years in private practice in Deep East Texas have been private in the strictest sense of the term. Although he's a proud member of the Sons of the Republic of Texas, as well as a number of other historical and preservation groups, and although he's been a registered architect for almost fifty years, he is not a member of the American Institute of Architects or either of its state or local components. "I'm not a sign-up man," says Raiford, who gives every indication of being instead a fiercely independent, proud, and stubborn cuss who believes in, as he puts it, "paddlin' his own canoe." Whereas preeminent Texas architect and San Antonio preservationist O'Neil Ford influenced others in part by traveling throughout the world and giving wonderful lectures, Raiford has kept pretty much to himself and taught mainly by example. As Austin architect and historian Eugene George says, "If there was a spotlight, Neil would jump into it; Raiford would always pull away into the shadows." Raiford's body of work, representing some of the most historic architecture in the state, speaks eloquently for itself, revealing far more than just the styles and technologies of various times. Through his projects run more than two hundred years of Texas history in all its glory, and in a way that no book or film could ever capture. And he is serious about it. Viewing the practice of architecture in general and historic preservation in particular as a sacred trust, Stripling approaches his work with a painstaking attention to detail and a tender appreciation of the soul of

a building that any archaeologist or Franciscan friar would admire.

Raiford's professional philosophies are traditional and pure. On design, that fundamental aspect of architecture that separates the artist from the engineer, he firmly embraces the Greek Revival style of the early to mid-nineteenth century, which so many of his finest restorations celebrate, and an interest that reflects to some extent his Beaux Arts training at Texas A&M. Although the style waned as a major influence on American architecture after the Civil War, Raiford's affinity for the Greek Revival still flavors the contemporary projects he designs from scratch (and which constitute most of his firm's work).

The Greek Revival is widely considered the last and most popular phase of the classical revival in American architecture that began in the late eighteenth century, when American architects as well as the founding fathers rebelled against all things English, including the Georgian style of architecture (a kind of "national style" created by English architects like Inigo Jones, James Gibbs, and Sir Christopher Wren and based on the writings of Italian Renaissance architect Andrea Palladio). Picking up on Palladio's idea of alluding to the architecture of classical Rome, Thomas Jefferson set out to create a completely new style of architecture for America—one that would not only look directly to ancient Greece and Rome for architectural inspiration but also symbolize the birth of the world's newest democracy. Jefferson's University of Virginia in Charlottesville (1826) and the U.S. Capitol in Washington (the central portion of which was completed in 1827 under the design direction of William Thornton and Charles Bulfinch)—considered classic examples of the Roman Revival in their use of Roman columns, domes, and vaults—paved the way for the additional use of columns, gabled roofs, pediments, and porticos that were distinctly Greek in origin (Greek and Roman features were often mixed in the same building).

During the first half of the nineteenth century, buildings that looked like great Greek temples were built in many major cities in America to house banks, churches, governmental bodies, libraries, and other institutions that benefited by projecting a certain image of solvency and solidity. As pattern books were published showing in detail the various orders and compositions of the style, house builders like Augustus Phelps in San Augustine and Abner Cook in Austin became well versed in Greek Revival design, which lent itself particularly well to mid-nineteenth-century Texas. By the Civil War, the Greek Revival had reached the middle of the state, describing the western boundary of the Old South (a line drawn north and south by Dallas, Waco, Austin, and San Antonio). As architectural historian Drury Blakeley Alexander points out, it was fairly easy to elaborate on a Texas farmhouse with Greek Revival parts and details, since the major feature of the style—the columnar porch—was common to most house types in the state, regardless of geographic or cultural origin. All a builder had to do was enlarge and make Doric or Ionic columns out of the posts that already supported the porch roof, add some molding, then top it all off with an entablature and simple cornice. "It brought a harmony and dignity to the simplest farm house," Alexander writes, "as well as elegance to the great mansion."[4]

What does Raiford see in the Greek Revival that makes it so timeless? "The clean lines, proportions, and details," he says, "as well as the beautiful balance and relation of the horizontal and vertical. The Greek Revival is not gaudy, but it does have some special features like jack arches, cornices, entablatures, pilasters, Palladian trim.

Visually, you have structural elements, whether they actually support anything or not."

Convinced that the Greek Revival is still a useful classic for just about any kind of building to allude to, Raiford is nevertheless reluctant to impose his design predilections on his clients, particularly for residential commissions. To him, the role of the architect in designing a house is not so much to dictate as it is to provide, and this role has brought him much satisfaction over the years. "I've always had a house going somewhere," Raiford says, "for a friend, or a friend of a friend. You help people out. The trick is to talk to the client enough to understand what he wants. You get to where you can interpret their needs and desires pretty easy. But it's always been my contention that that's an architect's purpose—helping people and making things look good. You try to read your client right, then when you get through, everybody's happy."

As for historic preservation, his real love and art, Raiford says you have to use your eyes. He remembers from his college days Dr. Mark Francis, who was dean of the A&M Veterinary School from 1916 to 1936. Back then, Raiford says, veterinary students used to tell how "Old Doc" Francis taught new classes to use their eyes in conjunction with their brains. Small and nattily dressed, he would stand before the class with a vessel full of liquid on his desk. "Now, I want you all to follow me and do as I do," he would say, dipping a finger in the liquid then pulling it out and sticking it into his mouth. The students would follow, one by one, until they had done exactly the same—or so they thought. When they were all back in their seats, Doc Francis would admonish the class: "Now, you see, you didn't do what I told you to do. I told you to use your eyes. That is horse piss," he would say, pointing to the vessel. "I put this finger in the horse piss, and *this* finger [a different one] in my mouth."

[4]Drury Blakeley Alexander, *Texas Homes of the 19th Century* (Austin: University of Texas Press, 1966), p. 85.

Using your eyes is equally important in preservation architecture, Raiford says, though it's not something you necessarily learn in school. It's a kind of developed expertise, a sensitivity sharpened on the job that enables you to know where to look and to know what you're looking at. And "if you don't react to what your eyes are telling you," Raiford says, "well, you better go back and take another look, because there's always evidence of something that happened, or needs to happen. You keep lookin'."

Raiford stresses the importance of keeping your mind open as well as your eyes, pointing out that there's always more than one possibility. "Don't have any preconclusions about anything," he says, "or you'll wind up in a mess. I tell you what, real positive people have a little trouble with preservation architecture. If you go and just absolutely commit yourself to something, you feel like you have to stay with it." It is important to keep in mind, he says, that preservation architecture takes as much patience and flexibility as anything else, "and as long as you keep an open mind, when you really find out the truth, and you can prove it, well, that's it. Don't ever say, 'This is the way it was,' or you're liable to make a mistake."

Raiford concedes that this can be hard for an architect, who is trained to create original designs and who would be inclined "just to go make a drawing and say this is it." There is very little certainty in preservation architecture. It may also be difficult for an architect to embrace the field in the first place as a truly creative calling. After all, in the restoration of a historic building, which mainly involves the repair and replication of original materials and features, who gets the design award? Would it be—posthumously perhaps—the architect who originally designed the building, or the restorationist, for his technical ability? It's a question often raised by design-award ju-

ries, but anyone who has ever been involved in the restoration of a building knows that, while original design may require more raw creativity, restoration requires more than just a mastery of the technical aspects of construction. In acquiring that mastery, preservation architects have to be imaginative problem solvers, and they develop a sensitive feel for historic styles, materials, tools, and craftsmanship that is unique among modern-day professions and trades. As Raiford says, "You get a *feelin'* for things."

Designing new buildings or restoring old ones, Raiford is convinced there is a common thread through it all that ties the past with the present and allows people to appreciate any kind of building, regardless of its style or when it was built. "Every age has a certain expression of itself," he says. "As long as you strive for quality. Built inside everyone is an appreciation of good proportions and good design. Human senses respond to that, whether it's in color or black and white, crossways or backwards."

Raiford's office is the top floor of the old San Augustine jail—a two-story red-brick box built in 1884 and situated in the lot behind Stripling's Drugstore, a town institution that fronts on Columbia, the main street. You enter the jailhouse through an eight-foot, steel-plate door that opens heavily into a small downstairs reception area. There is a desk by the stairway but no receptionist. ("We had one part-time a couple of years ago," Raiford says.) Along the north wall is a walnut cabinet stuffed with books— *The Story of Texas A&M*; *Ancient Greece*; *That Quail, Robert*; *Battles of Texas*—and old house parts—rusty hinges, shards of brick and pottery, pieces of columns and clapboard. A couch and coffee table are covered with shotgun shells and rumpled hunting clothes, and in one corner of the room two shotguns are propped muzzle down. On the walls are, for the most part, framed prints depicting various views of the Spanish Presidio La

Raiford heading toward his office in the old San Augustine jail. (Photograph by Dixon Daniel)

Bahía in Goliad, and by the stairway is a 1927 group photograph of an A&M cadet company. In it can be seen a gawky, jug-eared boy with a half grin on his face and big hands dangling from a tunic decidedly short in the sleeve. Upstairs, Raiford sits behind a desk awash in light from a window above it, the desk top completely covered with piles and scraps of paper. More La Bahía prints adorn the walls, along with all manner of photographs of family, buddies, and buildings. Three drafting tables and rolls of blueprints indicate this is a working architect's office, and a couch, easy chair, coffee table, refrigerator, and television betray it as also something of a home. And everywhere there are artifacts—more house parts, boyhood and career mementos—and ashtrays full of cigarette butts.

When giving a lecture at an architecture school or symposium somewhere, Raiford will often begin his talk by saying that Noah Webster defines two architects: Andrea Palladio and him. As it happens, the word *stripling* is Middle English for "one as thin as a strip," or, "a youth just passing from boyhood to manhood; a grown boy." It is one of our language's most accurate associations. Not particularly tall, Raiford has nevertheless been a long drink of water most of his life. He is lean and barrel chested, with big ears and hands and long arms, and often when he sits he will braid his long legs together like rope. He is usually dressed in something that suggests hunting—a corduroy shirt, say, with two quail embroidered on the breast pocket—and he is also somewhat famous for his headwear, a short-brimmed Borsalino sitting jauntily atop a head of smooth, silvery hair. Specks of blood on his baggy khaki pants show where he jabs himself in the thigh twice daily with an insulin needle, through the fabric. And his drawling speech is peppered with a mild blend of profanity and his own colloquialisms: "stabuena," a Stripling contraction of the Spanish *está buena* ("it is good"), or "blip, blip, blip," a kind of oral ellipses he uses to finish off a train of thought or belabored description.

Then there is an air of youthful dishevelment about Raiford, the way his clothes don't quite fit his frame, the way his habitats seem to have been formed by some great geologic upheaval. Whether in office, home, or automobile, Raiford exists in a world of material chaos, which belies his Beaux Arts expertise at carefully composing the elements of a building to make it look just right. It is perhaps this contradiction in his character—teenage haphazardness in his lifestyle, a sublime sense of order and proportion in his work—that makes him so rare; notwithstanding a certain flamboyance

Raiford in front of the Ezekiel Cullen House, San Augustine. (Photograph by J. Griffis Smith)

in his choice of hats, Raiford Stripling is a designer and restorer without pretense, and a kind of seventy-four-year-old boy.

But his youthful ways are almost always perceived through the wisp of a burning cigarette. Raiford smokes incessantly. Every ten minutes or so he will pluck a pack of Marlboros out of his shirt pocket and fire one up. He says he has smoked cigarettes since he was fifteen and that he has never tried to quit, or ever pronounced that he would. Although his life has been blunted by his smoking, Raiford nevertheless exhibits an irrepressible physical and mental stamina, able to work at his drawing board day and night if need be to get a job out on time. He also expresses an invigorating pleasure in people he knows and trusts.

When a hunting buddy drops by his office for a visit, Raiford will rise slowly from his drawing board, where he has hunkered for hours with his cigarettes and pencils, then spryly turn and greet his visitor with a brightness in his eyes and smile that makes you think he's going to break into a whooping country jig at any moment. Cigarettes have put wrinkles in his face that probably wouldn't have been there otherwise, in a way that cigarettes can do to a person, but the most obvious kinks in his physical makeup—weakening eyesight, a slowing gait—are due primarily to natural or accidental causes. Over the years, he has suffered from diabetes, arthritis, poor circulation, cataracts, detached retinas, perforated ulcers, broken ribs, and pinched nerves. He has also enjoyed the bottle to a great degree, but in 1964, when the doctor diagnosed diabetes and told him he would have to quit drinking, he gave it up just like that.

Through it all he has taken great delight in two all-consuming and completely unrelated passions: bird hunting and architecture. At the Institute of Texan Cultures in San Antonio in 1983, during a symposium in Raiford's honor, Texas A&M president Frank Vandiver asked in his opening remarks, "Did Raiford Stripling agree to be here because dove season is open in the central zone or because it is *not* open in the Rio Grande zone?" It was a good question, for anyone who knows Raiford knows that if he's not at his drawing board he would rather be hunting birds, or at least preparing a wild-game supper for friends or family. Later in the symposium, moderator Amy Freeman Lee recalled the first time she met Raiford, which was right before they began videotaping interviews for the symposium exhibit. "There were thirteen men and me in the room," she said, "and Raiford sat across the table and x-rayed me. Then Gordon Echols [A&M professor and symposium organizer] asked, 'When do we set up the filming?' And Raiford said, 'I'm not set-

tin' up anything as long as bird season is on.'" Later, Raiford called Lee to ask if she liked quail, which he was preparing for a dinner party that Lee was invited to attend. As it turned out, Lee—a consummate animal lover—indicated she liked quail far better on the wing than on the plate. She took a potato to bake and had a marvelous time. "I looked upon this," she said, "as a kind of spiritual challenge."

And whether tromping through a clearcut or a job site, Raiford has approached his task with the sort of pioneering obstinacy and strength that settled this part of the country in the first place. In Raiford, and in much of his setting, there is still a frontier ethos that manifests itself not only in the way people talk and dress but also in how they work and play and build their shelters. People are tough here, if not altogether ambitious or well-to-do. They make a living by cutting down and hauling trees to the pulp mills, they hunt deer and quail and coon, they worship God fundamentally, and, up until a few years ago, Raiford says, many of the old-timers in the woods still made and drank moonshine. In some ways they are very much like their pioneer progenitors—hard-bitten and fatalistic (if not always hankering to move toward a better life somewhere). Urban Texans who do battle in the corporate board room and racquetball court may consider themselves rugged individualists, but when it comes to living hard by the land and taking primitive pleasure in the fruits thereof, they couldn't hold a candle to a pioneer housewife, let alone the Raiford Striplings of this region.

Extracted from the wilderness, the stone, log, mud, and thatch that formed the first pioneer houses in Texas made for a vernacular of building that was as fundamental and sturdy as the people were. It was a primitive architecture, meeting the most basic needs of shelter with what the forest could provide before the sawmills and railroads could provide much of anything else—all this at a time when the Baroque was already wilting in Europe and refined tastes were turning back to the Greek and Roman classics. In 1826, when Milton Garrett was hammering the last square nail into his hand-hewn log house some ten miles outside of San Augustine, Thomas Jefferson's University of Virginia was nearing completion, and the central portion of the U.S. Capitol was a year from being finished.

On an important route for trade and immigration, however, San Augustine was not as isolated as many inland settlements, and even before Augustus Phelps introduced the notion of architectural style to its citizenry, there was a subtle sense of optimism and fashion in the folk architecture hereabouts. Settlers usually built the Disneyland caricature of a log cabin—structures made of perfectly round, saddle-notched logs—for use as temporary shelters while they constructed more substantial houses out of square logs. Each log would be hewn with a broadax or adz to a thickness of five to seven inches and made flat on the front and back, then connected at the corners with a more durable dovetail joint. Most important, the flat faces of the logs allowed for lapped siding to be applied when the sawmills came so the house would look like a civilized wood-frame house back East (though infinitely more durable). To cover up cracks between the logs on the inside, pioneer builders would rive out strips of wood about a half-inch thick on which paneling could eventually be nailed. Cracks on the outside would be chinked with a mixture of mud and Spanish moss.

House building in those days could also be very much a community effort. Before sawmills took the sweat out of turning raw timber into buildable boards, as Raiford points out with a certain anachronistic envy, few settlers ever started out to construct their cabins and barns all alone. The word would go out into the formative community that there was going to be a house raising, and people would come from miles around.

The women would cook and wash the pots and pans, and the men would fell trees in the virgin forest, size and notch the logs, and lay them up into a structure. Others would rive out the roof shingles and nailing strips, and the finish men would make the doors, door and window frames, and window blinds. The house raising was a social event, an occasion for isolated families to gather, gossip, work, and otherwise individually contribute to the welfare of the group. Later, as pioneer settlements became more established, log houses would be built by slaves or carpenters by trade, who would charge anywhere from twenty to seventy-five dollars, depending on the finish of the logs, number of rooms, size of the house, and type of wood.

In his research for the restoration of the Crocket House in San Augustine, Raiford found a reference in old man Crocket's notes to how fast a house raising could be accomplished before the first sawmill began operating in San Augustine County.[5] A man was serving on jury duty on Monday, and on Tuesday he heard that his house had burned down. He was excused from jury duty and went home, where his boys had already started riving out boards. So on Wednesday, Thursday, and Friday they had themselves a house raising, then on Saturday, the man moved his family into their new home. "Talk about modern conceptions of fast-track construction!" Raiford says with wonder.

---

[5] There is some disagreement about the date that happened. A historical marker claims that one of the earliest sawmills in Texas was built in what is now San Augustine County in 1819; another was built closer to town in 1825. Raiford, who has done more research on historic San Augustine than anyone alive, insists it was 1837; and George Crocket, citing deed records of San Augustine County, writes in *Two Centuries in East Texas* (p. 88) that the "earliest record of sawmills is to be found in an agreement in 1839 between Wyatt Hanks and Donald McDonald as owners, and John Murchison as engineer, to saw lumber of the Ayish Bayou, south of town, though the mill may have been running at an earlier date."

Still standing, the Milton Garrett House (see chapter 6) says as much about Raiford Stripling as it does about pioneer architecture. It is the oldest house in San Augustine County, one of the few nineteenth-century all-log houses in East Texas and as fine an example of pre-Republic architecture as you'll find anywhere in the state. Aware of its venerability for years, Raiford bought the house in 1969, when it was little more than a well-preserved heap of square logs and weathered gray siding on the road to Nacogdoches. He restored it to its original condition so that he could live in it, stooping to provide at least a few modern conveniences by turning a portion of the enclosed back porch into a bathroom, and it is now an uncanny reflection of the man who owns it—rough-hewn, honest, unadorned, and bearing all the marks of a life well spent.

Although Raiford has been unable to live in the house since an accident he had in 1982 (his 1967 T-bird was hit by a loaded logging truck as he pulled into the driveway), the Garrett House is still very much a Stripling dwelling place. Inside, hunting art by John P. Cowan hangs on almost every wall of the living room. Most of the prints show hunters in the field with their dogs, the hunters swinging their shotguns to follow quail rising from Johnson grass and goatweed with wings ablur, the dogs stiff on point with their tails sticking straight up. As in his jailhouse office-home in town, most of the wall space is covered with something framed. In addition to the Cowan prints there are prints and paintings of individual gamebirds and bird dogs, more paintings and sketches of La Bahía, photographs of friends and dignitaries. (Next to a photograph of hunting buddy Lea McKnight asleep in a chair are two photographs of Raiford with first ladies of the land: Eleanor Roosevelt at Mission Espíritu Santo in 1937 and Lady Bird Johnson at Presidio La Bahía in 1967.) On a wall by the front door hangs a giant 16-by-20½-inch photograph of Samuel Charles Phelps Vosper of New York sit-

Bust of Raiford at age twenty-three, sculpted by Hugo Villa.

ting at a dining table with a fork in one hand and a knife in the other, his head cocked to one side and his chubby face beaming at a birthday cake. Raiford took the photograph himself in Washington, D.C., in 1944. Upstairs in the "boys' room" (as it was called in Milton Garrett's day)—a half story running the full length of the house—there is a round poker table beneath a bare light bulb hanging from a beam, an old iron bed at one end, a bass fiddle leaning in a corner at the other. And in the southwest corner of the living room downstairs is a life-size bust of Raiford at the age of twenty-three. It was sculpted by Hugo Villa, a friend of Vosper and Raiford's who worked with Gutzon Borglum in pioneering the art of "sculpting by explosives" at Mount Rushmore. Made in a somewhat gentler fashion, the bust shows a smooth- and narrow-faced youth with a prominent forehead, firm jaw, slight underbite, and serious, intelligent eyes. It is easy to superimpose onto it the face of the older Raiford Stripling. You can see precisely where the wrinkles and sags have set in, and you can recognize the expression of "spirit" and "independence" that would be part of the title of the symposium held years later to honor Raiford's life and work: "Texas: A Sense of Place, a Spirit of Independence."

Embodying the very nature of his place and his passions, Raiford has become a legend, in a sense, in spite of himself—the small-town practitioner and non-joiner whose professional recognition has come as a by-product of his personal interests and pursuits. He has also gone against the grain of the preservation establishment in Texas from time to time, stubbornly insisting on a certain empirical approach that others have considered old-fashioned. In spite of his lifelong ability to make close and lasting friendships, Raiford has always had the makings of a loner who didn't like to be told what to do; he has simply done what he thought was right, whether it resulted in criticism or praise. In any case, he seems more proud of having been inducted into the Knights of the Order of San Jacinto, knighted in the Alamo with Sam Houston's own sword, than he is of just about anything he's ever done.

But Raiford is a legend, of course, mainly because of himself. Anyone who knows him knows that he is honorable and generous to a fault, a man who holds faster to his word than to his money. Then there is always something intriguing about a professional man—particularly the practitioner of such an urban specialty as architecture—who returns to his small-town home after going off to college and being exposed to worldly people and ideas. Disciplined by his Beaux Arts training and professionally nurtured by a master designer, Raiford did come home again, and for all of his career he has proved the adage that you may be able to take the boy out of the country for a while, but you can never take the country out of the boy, any more than you can take the boy out of the man. Above all, as his sister Frances points out, Raiford Stripling has a "quiet dignity and knowledge of what he is about." Exploring the roots of Texas building traditions, it is clear that the indigenous architecture in this state is the better for Raiford's understanding of himself and of his art. And it is equally plain to see that the architects of today's urban Texas would do well to study the forms and features that he has so lovingly preserved and sought to perpetuate.

CHAPTER 2

Provenance

THE Striplings first came to East Texas from Georgia around 1850 after a stay in Nachobe County, Mississippi, settling in a farm community in Nacogdoches County called Forks of the River. Abner and his son Benjamin were listed in the census as "mechanics," which meant—in the days before the internal combustion engine—that they made wagons and barrel staves. The family also farmed, raising cotton, corn, sorghum, and sugar cane on sixty-two acres of Angelina River bottomland, which they cleared of virgin timber in three years and which is now well under the Sam Rayburn Reservoir. As a soldier in the Confederate army, Benjamin Stripling escaped from the siege of Vicksburg in 1863 and walked all the way across Louisiana to get back home. He died in September of 1880, five months before the birth of his last child, Raiford Nichols, who came to be called "Raif." Two months after Raif was born, his mother, Narcissa Johnson Stripling, also died, leaving him to be reared by his only sister, Frances "Fannie" Ivey, and two of his older brothers, Sam and Bob.

Life in Forks of the River in the 1880s, as elsewhere in rural America, could be hard and brief. Families were large not only because of ineffective measures of birth control but also because offspring provided a ready supply of labor, which placed a premium on boys—lots of them. Families could always count on losing some sooner or later—by accident, illness, or violence. Of ten boys and one girl in the Stripling family, born over a twenty-eight-year period, two boys died of typhoid fever before they reached their teens, and two others didn't make it to thirty.

In the 1880s, the magnetism of the West still pulled settlers in that direction, and hearing that good cotton land in West Texas was plentiful and cheap, the Striplings loaded everything they owned into an ox-drawn wagon, with dogs and cows tied to the back, and headed west. It is said that Bob's wife, Aunt "Zoo" (Missouri Axley before she wed), made lye soap along the way. And whether an indication of their homesickness or the arrangement of the wagon seats, all the riders sat facing east the entire trip.

The Striplings didn't stay very long. Disappointed in the land (due in part, perhaps, to the geographical shock they must have felt in moving from piney woods to arid plains inside a single state), the family soon returned to Nacogdoches County. In 1893, when Raif was twelve, his beloved sister Fannie died, and the younger siblings were parceled out to various older brothers. Raif

Ben and Narcissa Stripling, Raiford's grandparents.

stayed a while in Forks with cousin Roxie and brother Jake, then moved to Melrose to live with his brother Bob, who had a farm there. In 1898, when he was seventeen, Raif moved to Nacogdoches at the behest of brother Sam, who got him a job for fifteen dollars a month in Perkins Drug washing out beer bottles from an upstairs saloon so they could be reused to hold medicine. Meanwhile, Jake developed tuberculosis, went out to New Mexico for his health, then rode a bicycle to Oklahoma, where he settled down and married and wound up running a grocery store in Edmond. (Sam would prosper in the drug

business in Nacogdoches and would eventually rear five children, one of whom, Mack Stripling, would attend law school at the University of Texas in the 1930s— where he roomed with John Connally— and return to Nacogdoches to practice law, serve as mayor, and eventually own a bank.) Brother John earned a degree from Sam Houston State College (now Sam Houston State University) in Huntsville and went on to serve in the Texas legislature around the turn of the century. The widower John Ivey, Fannie's husband, continued to follow his calling as a Baptist preacher.

After three years of washing out beer

bottles at Perkins Drug, Raif was ready for something better. By the time he was twenty, his brother Sam was a partner in the Stripling-Hazelwood Drug Company in Nacogdoches, and he hired Raif on as a kind of pharmacist's apprentice. Although he only had an eighth-grade education, Raif was bright and diligent, and by the time he was twenty-two, he had passed his licensing exam to become a registered pharmacist.

Still languishing after the 1890 fire that destroyed its business district, San Augustine—thirty-five miles southeast of Nacogdoches—needed all the help it could get. Even before the fire, the railroads had pushed on to Nacogdoches and Lufkin, by-passing San Augustine and leaving the once-bustling center of commerce and culture to wither on the vine. Local historian George L. Crocket writes of cotton wagons driving through the streets of the town, "bound for distant markets, without even stopping to invite a bid."[1] Then in 1900, the Santa Fe railroad extended its Beaumont-Longview line right through San Augustine, and the town gained a new lease on life. "It was as if," Crocket writes, "the new century marked the beginning of a new era."[2] New downtown buildings went up, new businesses were established, and cotton and timber became king again, with gins and mills and planer plants opening up throughout the county. This boom would be short-lived, ending with the Great Depression in the thirties, but it did lend some excitement to the county for the time being, and some appeal to out-of-town businessmen who saw some opportunity there.

In 1903, when he was twenty-two, Raif heard that the only drugstore in San Augustine, destroyed by the 1890 fire, had

never reopened. Concerned as much about the lack of pharmaceutical services for the people of San Augustine County as he was excited by potential profits, Raif rode to San Augustine in a one-horse mail cart to look the situation over. It looked sufficiently promising, and on January 10, 1904, he joined with local merchant John B. Burrows to establish the San Augustine firm of Stripling and Burrows, specializing in the dispensing of prescription drugs.

In the remembrances of his sons and daughters, it is said with much affection that Raiford Nichols Stripling was a very fine man, one of San Augustine's greatest, at par with some of the town's most illustrious early citizens. At twenty-two, Raif came to San Augustine with a grand vision and heart, and he lived a long, fruitful, and compassionate life there. As the new druggist in town, he rode all over the county on horseback, carrying a satchel full of quinine, calomel, and other remedies for people who couldn't get to town on a regular basis. And if they couldn't pay cash either, Raif accepted sweet potatoes, watermelons, and chickens, which the people could drop off at the drugstore when they did make it in. He never refused medicine to anybody who needed it, and when people came knocking on the door in the middle of the night, with a sick child in their arms, he got up and went to the store and gave them whatever the doctor had prescribed.

Raif was to be best known, perhaps, for serving twenty-six years as San Augustine County judge, during which he tirelessly campaigned for better roads, faster mail delivery, and rural electrification. Even as a private citizen during the Great Depression, which hit East Texas hard, Raif developed his "Five-Year Betterment Program" for the county, urging people to plant gardens, clean up their property, and beautify their cemeteries. He also organized community meetings all over the county, taking two of his daughters along for entertainment.

[1] George Louis Crocket, *Two Centuries in East Texas: A History of San Augustine County and Surrounding Territory from 1685* (San Augustine: Christ Episcopal Church, 1932), p. 350.
[2] Ibid., p. 351.

(They had had "expression" in school, Frances recalls, and could tap dance and sing.) In 1937 Raif was instrumental in organizing the seven-county Deep East Texas Electric Cooperative, serving as its first president, and when he was eighty and attending an REA convention in Washington, he tried to generate support for making El Camino Real a national parkway from Washington to Mexico. His appreciation for modern roadways was a vicarious one, since he had never learned to drive a car, but he was progressive in his outlook in every other way. (There is no small irony in the fact that, as a man who believed in progress in the days when old houses could be considered more trouble than they were worth, Raif was partly responsible for the demise of two of the most historic homes in San Augustine County, the Horton House and the Henderson House.) "My father did more for the poor and underprivileged people in San Augustine County than anyone before or since," says his youngest son Robert. He was also dapper and active to the last, showing up at the drugstore every morning in coat and tie. He died August 31, 1978, at the age of ninety-seven, his face as slick as a baby's, according to Robert, and with all his original teeth.

In spite of his big and generous heart, Raif was also a pretty good businessman, and he managed to establish a prosperous enterprise in Stripling and Burrows. In 1905, the firm moved into a new two-story brick building, with a doctor's office on the second floor, on the northwest corner of Columbia and Harrison streets. Stripling and Burrows cleared $32,000 its first year, and soon had branch stores in Bronson, Texas, and Santa Fe, New Mexico. It also had one of the best soda fountains in East Texas, complete with two full-time soda jerks and eight flavors of Dairyland ice cream. Milk for the drugstore was furnished by a dozen registered jersey milk cows that grazed on Stripling land outside of town. Raif

eventually bought out Burrows, who had wanted to expand into the wholesale grocery business, and just before World War I the establishment became Stripling's Drugstore, which moved into its present location in 1934.

No small part of Raif's early success as a pharmacist was due to his marriage, on August 3, 1909, to Winfrey Robbie Leak, daughter of a doctor in nearby Center, up in Shelby County. The Leaks had also come to East Texas from Georgia in 1849 or 1850, as the Striplings had done, but the two families were of different persuasions. The Leaks came from a long line of physicians and could trace their lineage to thirteenth-century France. The surname Leak, in fact, is thought to have come from the French word for leech, which medieval doctors used in treating their hapless patients. Destined for a more scientific approach to medicine, the family (whose surname was originally spelled de Lec) could have come to England from Normandy as early as 1208, and in the 1600s a number of Leakes (as the name was then commonly spelled) migrated to America, with one branch settling in Virginia and another in Georgia.

Dr. Robert Leak, born April 12, 1825, in Rome, Georgia, came to Texas by ship around 1849 with his wife Mary Ann Gilder and six slaves, settling in Melrose, between Nacogdoches and San Augustine on the Old Natchez–San Antonio Trace, or King's Highway. Until a year before his retirement at seventy-four, Dr. Leak had his office in a large upstairs room of his home, a grand two-story plantation house made of hand-hewn timber with dovetail joints, wood pegs, and square nails and located at the fork of the upper and lower Melrose roads. It has become something of a family joke that the good doctor didn't want to see anyone who was too sick to make it up the stairs. He would, however, take his practice to the people. Dr. Leak was his own pharmacist, and, like his grandson-in-law Raif

Stripling, he traveled by horseback or buggy to treat patients in the county who couldn't come to town. And from those who couldn't pay cash, he accepted produce, lard, and ribbon-cane syrup.

Dr. Leak had graduated from Atlanta Medical College, as would three of his sons: Dr. Robert Arlington Leak (1852–83), Dr. Erastus Ellington Leak (1855–1920), and Dr. Mitchel G. Leak (1860–91). A fourth son, D. A. Leak, was a Christian minister. Before setting up his practice in Center, Dr. E. E. Leak married Lillian Pearl Blakey, and of this union was born a daughter, Winfrey Robbie Leak, on March 13, 1888. Winfrey's mother also had a proud ancestry. Spearheading a lineage that went back to the Magna Charta, Churchill Blakey, Lillian's great-great-great-grandfather, had come to America from England in the 1600s, settling in Virginia and serving in its House of Burgesses.

Returning to San Augustine from a honeymoon trip to San Francisco, Denver, and Santa Fe, Raif and Winfrey Stripling set out to build a family as well as a business. As it happened, they ended up building "two families." Raiford Leak Stripling was born November 23, 1910, his brother Robert two years later. Seven years would pass before Frances was born, followed by Sarah, Martha, and Mary Jane—each separated by about two years. The effect was a somewhat disjointed brood, divided by sex as well as age, but family life was close and loving. If Raiford seemed more like an uncle than a brother to youngest sister Mary Jane (he was fifteen when she was born), he was an exceptionally good one. The girls always looked up to Raiford and valued his connection to their lives, whether he was taking Frances along for the ride in their mother's Oldsmobile as he and Robert delivered papers around town, barely able to see over the dash, or sending an evening dress to Frances as a gift out of the blue when she was a student at the University of Texas. "I

Raiford (*right*), his brother Robert, and their father Raif (ca. 1913).

could not have dreamed," Frances says, "of a more wonderful big brother than Raiford."

Between 1900 and 1929, San Augustine wasn't a bad place for a boy to grow up, particularly if he had proprietary access to one of the best soda fountains in East Texas. It was a good, almost privileged life for Raiford and Robert. The drugstore featured not only eight flavors of Dairyland ice cream but also sixteen full-time clerks, who sold everything from auto parts to fine jewelry. The resident watch tinker was the official watch repairman in that area for the Santa Fe Railroad. And although he didn't drive a lick, Raif had a fleet of five cars and trucks. He also employed a black cook named Chester who made the noon meal at home. A firm believer that every boy should know how to plow and cut wood and generally be indus-

trious with his time, Raif Stripling nevertheless allowed his sons a wide and carefree
rein. Raiford and Robert rode horses with
Press Kelly and King Roberts, who tended
Mr. Stripling's cattle, drove automobiles up
and down the red logging roads, played
marbles with the prized Bavarian agates
their father would bring back from Cullum
and Boren in Dallas, hunted game in the
fields and forests, and swam in every "wash
hole" in the county. Raiford also did all
those things with Americus Holman "Top"
Cartwright, a close friend from boyhood
on and the great-grandson of Matthew
Cartwright, whose Phelps-built house in
San Augustine Raiford would restore years
later. According to Raiford, he and his
brother learned to drive when Raiford was
eight or nine by blackmailing their father's
deliveryman, one of the Garner boys, who
would slip off every night in the drugstore
delivery truck to visit his girlfriend in the
black quarter. Robert found out about it,
and he and Raiford offered to keep it a se-
cret in exchange for driving lessons. When
Raiford was eleven and Robert nine, their
father gave them a car, a stripped-down
Model-T Ford they called a "hoopie." Neither one of them was big enough to crank it,
Raiford recalls, so they would always park
it on an incline, with chocks in front of
the tires, and roll it to a start when the
need arose. Introduced to guns and wildlife
by an uncle, William Jenkins (their father
wasn't much of an outdoorsman), they
loved to hunt more than anything, first with
slingshots, then with BB guns, and when
Raiford was twelve his father gave him a
twenty-eight-gauge shotgun. Thus began a
lifelong affair with the art of shooting birds
on the wing with a shotgun and the loyal assistance of a dog. Asked in a television interview once if he had any "marks of dis-
tinction," Raiford said he did indeed: he
had owned a bird dog continuously since
he was eight years old. "As I have so often
said," says his younger brother Robert, "I

don't believe anyone had a better childhood
than Mr. Stripling's two boys."

One of Raiford's best hunting buddies as
a boy—and throughout most of their lives—
was a black man fourteen years his senior
named Peter Payne. Peter was best known
for his talent on the ball field, serving out an
entire hitch in the army during World War I
playing baseball in San Antonio, but around
San Augustine he was even more famous
for shooting a shotgun and training bird
dogs. When he got out of the army he returned to San Augustine and went to work
at Stripling's Drugstore, doing what Raif
had done as a boy for his brother at Perkins
Drug in Nacogdoches—washing bottles.
Peter says whenever Raiford came into the
drugstore he would badger him to take him
hunting, and Peter would oblige, showing
Raiford how to shoot, carry, and be safe
with his shotgun and often carrying young
Raiford on his back through the high grass
to keep him from being covered in cockle-
burs. Raiford would come to call Peter "the
professor of the bird-dog academy," for
Peter probably knew more about bird dogs
than anybody in the county. Raiford would
bring him puppies—mostly pointers and
setters—and Peter would train and tend
them at his house, sometimes keeping as
many as twenty dogs out in back.

Growing up together as the first phase of
the Stripling brood, Raiford and Robert
were also pretty good buddies. Robert never
had to wear Raiford's hand-me-downs, Robert says, and the two boys hardly ever
fought. At times, however, there was a certain pesky competitiveness in their relationship, and older brother Raiford could be
downright ornery. The summer Robert was
twelve he came down with typhoid fever,
which several people in San Augustine had
died of, and for a week or so he lay near
death. No one entered his room except his
mother and the doctor. One of the possible
complications of typhoid fever is intestinal
hemorrhage or perforation, and treatment

in Robert's day usually included a liquid diet. Robert's hunger became so intense, he recalls, that his mother censored every image of food from his reading material, although she did wrap fresh bread in linen napkins from time to time and bring it in for Robert just to smell. Raiford, however, had his own ideas for Robert's therapy. In Raiford's defense, Robert says his older brother—all of fourteen at the time—had no idea how seriously ill his younger brother really was, but after lunch each day Raiford would bring a piece of pie or cake to Robert's door, which Raiford would crack open just enough for Robert to watch him slowly eat the dessert, licking his chops with satisfaction.

Then there was the summer that Raiford and Robert rode so much with Press Kelly and King Roberts that poor Robert got "galled" between his legs, chafed "raw as beefsteak." Standing bow-legged in the barn after a long day's ride, Robert asked his older brother what he should do about it, and Raiford advised him to take a good bath and then liberally apply some Sloan's Liniment on the affected parts. Raiford then reached up and got a bottle of Sloan's off a shelf and handed it to Robert. In those days, Sloan's Liniment came in two strengths— one for people, one for farm animals, and the latter was considerably more potent. Robert followed his older brother's sage advice, he recalls, and "it was just as if someone had lit two blow torches to my crotch." He ran screaming from the house and, after a wild chase, was eventually caught by his parents, who had no idea what had happened. When they found out, Robert says, "the galling between my legs was nothing compared to Ray's butt when my father got through with him. Ray knew what would happen; he just thought it would be a good joke. It was, but it damn near killed us both."

Raiford had a way with a pencil as well as his mischievous wits, and when he was in the second grade he discovered he could draw. "I just had the ability," he says. "I could do it, and I started doin' it." Saved and surely cherished by his mother over the years, one of Raiford's earliest works—a small woodcut of Abraham Lincoln for his grammar-school paper *The Wild Rose*—rests on a shelf in his artifact-cluttered office. The image was probably copied from a picture, but it is an exceptionally good likeness of Abe Lincoln, particularly for the hands of a fifth-grader with a pocketknife.

Aware of his artistic talent at an early age, Raiford nevertheless gave little indication as a youth that he wanted to become an artist or an architect. He did not spend all his time drawing houses in the margins of his notebooks, nor did he spend it all with his nose in his textbooks. He was allowed to skip the third grade because of a shortage of space and a surplus of third-graders in San Augustine that year, and because he was a quick learner and could make the advancement with ease. "Raiford was very smart in school," Robert recalls, "even though he didn't seem to study very much." Robert also remembers that throughout their growing-up years, he had no idea that Raiford wanted to be an architect. Raiford's childhood interests were broad and unquenchable, among them a keen curiosity about Texas history that was encouraged by local historian George L. Crocket, who was also Raiford's scoutmaster and the pioneer vicar of San Augustine's Christ Episcopal Church. Raiford grew up particularly conscious of Texas' involvement in the Civil War, the bitterness of which still lingered around every courthouse square in East Texas. There were a few old battlefields in the region, and Raiford remembers visiting one with his grandfather near Old Sabine Town and finding a cannonball that he still has in his office somewhere. When he was ten years old, Raiford was far more interested in being a ten-year-old in the wilds of East Texas than in fulfilling some naive dream of being a professional man someday.

His mother had more specific hopes for her oldest son. Winfrey Leak Stripling, one of the few women of her day who had been to college (Southwestern University in Georgetown, 1906–1907), was a well-bred, strong-willed lady of the Old South, and she wanted her oldest son to continue the professional tradition on her side of the family and become a doctor. To that end, Raiford recalls, she worked on him night and day, and her desires were not easily deflected. As Raif spent more and more time at the drugstore (which was open seven days a week) or serving his beloved community, Winfrey became the dominant figure of the family, the loving disciplinarian who could exact obedience from her sons without instilling fear. She was also a staunch Methodist, and as long as the boys lived at home, they had to be staunch Methodists, too—attending church every Sunday, studying their lessons in Sunday school, singing in the choir. "Until we got away from home," Raiford says, "anything that happened at church we were in it."

Not that the boys obeyed her every command to the letter. In 1920, when the whole town turned out for what was to be San Augustine's last hanging, Winfrey Stripling refused to let her boys attend. Being boys, of course, they tried to see it anyway, scampering to the top of the barn roof to view the execution four blocks away—a black man hanged for shooting a white man and woman (and killing neither one). "We were under Mama's domain at home," Raiford says, "but she was real simpatico with us." Nevertheless, always feeling more like a Stripling than a Leak, Raiford considered himself "Papa's boy," and under the spell of his talents as an artist and his knack for learning, Raiford went about his childhood like anybody else, waiting for just the right experience to come along and set him on his way.

Although Raiford's mother was a lady of the Old South, who required blacks to enter her home only through the back door, she did foster a close and lasting bond between Raiford and Robert and a black boy named Eddie Phillips. The Striplings took Eddie in when he was orphaned, built him a little house in back, and raised him with their own. The three boys grew very close, and in later years, according to Robert, Eddie would come to Raiford's rescue more times than either could count, exerting an immeasurable influence on Raiford's life. Until his death in the early sixties, Eddie served as a kind of retainer for Raiford, a combination chauffeur, valet, bird-dog tender, chief bottle washer, counselor, and confidant. "Eddie was indeed a member of our family," Robert says, "and, like my father, was one of the finest men I have ever known. I have often said that he was just like my brother, except I thought I liked Eddie the most."

In the summer of 1924, encouraged by their father to make something of it, Raiford and Robert cultivated a tomato patch across the street from the courthouse square that had once been a trading lot for horses and mules. Due to the fecundity of the soil as well as the industriousness of the Stripling boys, the patch produced an abundance and quality of tomatoes that made Raiford and Robert famous throughout the county. It also won Raiford first prize in a local contest sponsored by the 4-H Club and the Santa Fe Railroad, which was a trip by train to Chicago to attend the great Chicago Livestock Exhibition.

It was a trip to be remembered, consisting of many firsts. Especially for the occasion, Raiford's mother bought him his first pair of long pants. (Until then, as most boys did in those days, he had worn only knickers and black stockings.) It was also the first time he had ever left Texas and the first time he had ever visited a truly big city. And it was the first time Raiford had ever traveled on a train in a special car with eighteen other boys and box after box of Texas figs and

Texas boys at the Chicago Livestock Exhibition in 1924. Raiford is in the front row, sixth from right. Shepherding the group was (*far left*) Sterling Evans, later president of the Texas A&M Board of Directors.

pink grapefruit, which sponsors were sending along to interest Chicagoans in Texas produce. It was a good idea having them hand out figs and grapefruit at a Chicago livestock show, but it made for a raucus return trip. On the way back, Raiford remembers, "we were pullin' ever' kinda devil in the world we could think about on that train." Inevitably, all the leftover grapefruit wound up being used as projectiles in one long-running battle, during which one special railcar was practically torn apart by nineteen indefatigable Texas boys.

It is altogether fitting, writes Katy Capt in her monograph on Raiford, that Chicago was the first big city that Raiford ever experienced.[3] A fertile seedbed of architectural theory and practice, the city most recently had staged the World's Columbian Exposition of 1893, which did much to replace the romantic Victorian styles of the late nineteenth century with a revival of classical formality that struck the public fancy. Chicago architect Louis Sullivan and others of the

[3] Katy Capt, "Raiford Leak Stripling: The Life and Times of an East Texas Restoration Architect" (master's thesis, Texas A&M University, 1981), p. 6.

Chicago school had also just pioneered the steel-frame skyscraper, made possible by the elevator and sporting a sinuous Art Nouveau–like ornament. If Raiford was toting figs and pink grapefruit to Chicago on more of an agricultural mission than anything else, he was also firming up certain professional predilections about his future. Touring the Marshall Field store and Union Stockyards and the McCormick tractor plant made vivid impressions on young Raiford, but there was something about the LaSalle Hotel, where the boys stayed, that impressed him even more.

For one thing, it was the tallest building Raiford had ever been in. Designed by the prominent Chicago firm Holabird and Roche and built in 1909, the LaSalle (since demolished) rose twenty-two stories from the northwest corner of LaSalle and West Madison streets, the very heart of Chicago's financial district. It was one of the finest hotels in the city, featuring an ornate exterior of molded granite, rusticated ashlar, brick, buff terra cotta, and glazed green tile. Designed in a Louis XIV vein and named after the French explorer, the building was also topped with a curving mansard roof and contained a wealth of public spaces and services inside, from opulent dining and banquet rooms to newsstands and telephone booths. The LaSalle was like a town unto itself, and with 1,172 guest rooms—each of which had hot and cold running water—it could lavish its luxuries on almost the entire population of San Augustine, which numbered 1,268 in 1920. Raiford and his pals all stayed on the fourteenth floor, which afforded an unforgettable view of downtown Chicago. For a thirteen-year-old East Texas boy in the days before commercial air travel, such a vantage point also made it hard for Raiford to ignore the fact that he was higher than he had ever been in his life. "I would often look out the window," he says, "just to look down and see how far in the hell it was to the ground."

Raiford returned to San Augustine with a pretty good idea of what he wanted to be when he grew up, and it wasn't a doctor. To his mother's minor disappointment, Raiford set his sights on architecture—something he had only read about before his Chicago trip and that he could now see as a tangible, productive way for an adult to be creative. Drawing or painting, although he saw it as a good form of personal expression, simply hadn't interested him as a career, perhaps because there is rarely a living in it. Nor did Raiford seem to have the temperament to express himself on paper or canvas and leave it at that. But designing buildings, now *that* was a substantive livelihood! Although few architects ever get rich just by practicing architecture, they can make a decent living by envisioning and drawing. And—perhaps most important—their visions are actually built and used. Raiford's decision was reinforced by the arrival in town, in the mid-twenties, of Tyler architect Shirley Simons, a Beaux Arts designer par excellence who was commissioned to do some work around the square and who would later design the new San Augustine County Courthouse, built in 1927. Raiford's father once introduced him to Simons, and although Raiford knew of the work that the Page brothers from Austin had done in town—his elementary school, a bank—Simons was the first real live architect he ever knowingly laid eyes on.

Winfrey shifted her desire for a physician son over to Robert, and Raiford—a year ahead of his age group and attending a high school that went only to the eleventh grade—was free to be whatever he wished. If he wanted to be an architect, his father reasoned, then he should plan on going to Rice Institute in Houston, Shirley Simons's alma mater and, under the direction of eminent architectural educator William Ward Watkin, the home of a very fine school of architecture. "The fact of the matter is," Raiford says, "he bribed me, said he'd get me a

Ford convertible if I'd go to Rice." But Raiford had other plans. Not only had he been impressed with Shirley Simons and his work, but Raiford had also been influenced and inspired by his young high-school agriculture teacher, R. F. McSwain, a recent graduate of the Agricultural and Mechanical College of Texas (now Texas A&M University) and his sponsor for the prize-winning tomato patch on the courthouse square. As Katy Capt writes, "Such success under McSwain's tutelage could do little but increase his stature in Stripling's eyes."[4]

Disappointing both of his parents, in a sense, and sharing little of his career plans with his brother, Raiford aimed himself toward architecture school at A&M when he was a junior in high school, eventually graduating as the salutatorian of his high-school class in May of 1927. His mind was made up, and there was precious little anybody could do about it. Meanwhile, he continued to excel in school as well as carouse in his spare time. When he wasn't exercising his persuasive powers on the debate team or playing the saxophone in the band, Raiford and his buddy J. P. "Pete" Mathews would go over to nearby Hemphill "to do a little courtin'," which they often subsidized by "kiting"—writing counter checks at the grocery store in Hemphill when they didn't really have the money to cover them, then beating the checks back to the bank in San Augustine, where Mathews's older brother worked as a cashier. As Mathews recalls, each check never amounted to more than $1

or $1.50, enough to cover a night on the town in those days, and the boys would always make good on the checks so they could continue the practice.

Raiford and Pete also played on the high-school baseball team, Raiford in center field, Pete behind the plate. Always on the gangly side, Raiford had a hard time convincing the coach that he would make a good ballplayer. But he was eager to try, and he persuaded the coach to give him a chance. To demonstrate his ability, Raiford was first assigned to right field, which was bounded by a barbed-wire fence. There was an understanding on the team that if anyone hit a ball that far, the right fielder didn't have to play it and risk being entangled in barbed wire. Most of the boys gladly abided by that, but not Raiford, who was so determined to make the team, he wasn't about to let any barbed wire get in the way. So one day, scrambling after a fly ball that would have easily gone over the fence, he succeeded in catching it, but not without plunging himself into the barbed wire and being lacerated from head to toe. As his brother Robert tells the tale, the coach was ready to send Raiford to the doctor when Raiford insisted on keeping his turn at bat. "He got up at the plate looking like a side of beef and actually got a hit," Robert says. "He made the team all right, but even today he can show you the scars from his encounter with the fence. He was and still is very determined in anything he undertakes. In fact, his friends called him 'Hammer,' for hammerhead. Raiford has always been just plain damn hardheaded."

[4]Capt, "Raiford Leak Stripling," p. 6.

CHAPTER 3

Bayonets and Smocks

THE Agricultural and Mechanical College of Texas opened its doors on October 4, 1876, with the idea of offering a first-rate vocational education to young Texas men not bound by privilege for a private, classical education back East. As was common in those days, particularly among schools in the South, the curriculum was fashioned around a military regimen, which was designed to inculcate such virtues as discipline, honor, and leadership and to bolster the national defense. That the curriculum was directed toward "the sons of toil" at the apparent exclusion of its daughters was not a conscious plot against the young women of the state; farming, engineering, and soldiering were considered decidedly unfeminine by men and women alike in the nineteenth century, and few women ever went to college anyway.

Although A&M was a men's academy, for all practical purposes, it was also a product of an idea proposed by Johnathan B. Turner at Illinois College in 1850 that did more to democratize American education than anything before or since (with the possible exception of the G.I. Bill of Rights a century later). The idea was indeed revolutionary: No longer should college be the exclusive province of the upper classes, Turner argued. Higher education should be made available to the "industrial classes" as well, and instead of grounding the students solely in the classics, they should also become well versed in the "practical arts." This revolutionary notion was picked up (some say first conceived) by Sen. Justin S. Morrill of Vermont, who introduced the bill in Congress that resulted in the Land-Grant College Act of 1862. This act set aside thousands of acres of public land across the country for the states to sell so as to invest the proceeds in a permanent fund, the interest from which would then be used to set up and operate a land-grant college (but not to construct or maintain its buildings). States were given five years from the date of the act to establish a college "where the leading subject shall be, without excluding other scientific and classical studies, and including military tactics, to teach such branches of learning as are related to agriculture and the mechanic arts . . . in order to promote the liberal and practical education of the industrial classes in the several pursuits and professions of life."[1]

By the time Texas returned to the Union in 1865, becoming eligible for the benefits of the federal land-grant act, the state's legis-

[1] Henry C. Dethloff, *A Centennial History of Texas A&M University 1876–1976* (College Station: Texas A&M University Press, 1975), I, xi.

lators had already explored the feasibilities of creating a public land-grant institution as well as a state agricultural college, in addition to a central "University of Texas," which had been established on paper in 1858 with legislation that also set aside 221,420 acres of land for its sustenance. But there was no legislative consistency as to how this state system of higher learning should be structured, or even if it should be a "system" at all. One bill called for two public universities, another designated only one. The state constitution of 1876 specified A&M College as a "branch of The University of Texas," but the college was to operate as an independent institution governed by a separate board of directors.[2]

All this confusion over A&M's status was critical to its founders not only because of its academic identity but also—even more important, as it would turn out—because of its claim to a portion of the revenues from the 221,420 acres given for the "establishment and endowment of two colleges or Universities" by the Fourth Texas Congress in 1839. Later, in addition to specifying A&M as a "branch of The University of Texas," the constitution of 1876 added one million acres to the university land endowment, and the legislature granted another million in 1883, for a grand total (after settling claims and correcting inaccurate surveys) of 2.1 million acres. The income from this land, which came mostly from leasing and selling portions of it without the mineral rights, came to be known as the Permanent University Fund, and although the two schools haggled for years over their fair share, it never really amounted to much.

Then on Monday morning, May 28, 1923, drilling into university land near the small West Texas town of Big Lake, a discovery well called Santa Rita No. 1 blew in, and the Permanent University Fund became a hot property. By 1926, oil royalties from the Big

Lake field amounted to $250,000 per month. Quickened now by the oil boom and the swelling university fund, negotiations over A&M's rightful share of it continued in good faith but with little resolution. Nevertheless, even though there was still disagreement over how it should be divided, the fund had accumulated $5 million in oil royalties in just three years, and the future looked undeniably bright for both institutions.

A&M College was indeed at a turning point in 1926. Not only did the oil boom promise to enrich its coffers, but a host of other issues and concerns also contributed to a portentous turbulence that would thrust the college into its second half century. Since its founding in 1876, seven years before the first class was actually held at the University of Texas in Austin, A&M College had been a small campus oriented west toward the railroad tracks, where its students were delivered from all across Texas. It was a symbolic orientation as well as a physical one. Established on the flat, scrubby plain of the Brazos River Valley as the West was being won, the college was a kind of academic outpost where a student body of less than a thousand drilled and studied and fended off the scorpions, pumas, and wolves. By the end of World War I, in which it gloriously took part, A&M was a different place. As the first college to offer its facilities to the federal government for war training, by March 1918 A&M had a larger percentage of its graduates in the service than any other college or university in the United States. One half of the men who had graduated from A&M since its founding fought in World War I, and forty-nine A&M soldiers died as a result of it. When the war ended and the veterans came back, enrollment expanded rapidly. In 1919 it was 50 percent higher than in any previous year, although the legislature was hard pressed to appropriate enough money to expand the campus accordingly. Of all the Texas high-school graduates in 1923 who went on to college,

[2] Ibid., p. 7.

one-third enrolled at A&M, where three hundred students were sleeping in tents.

What new arrivals found when they stepped off the train in the fall of 1925 was a physical plant consisting of forty-one permanent buildings on 10,208 acres of ground, and during the 1925–26 term, the total enrollment was 2,379, taught by a faculty of 193. Thomas Otto Walton succeeded William Bennett Bizzell as president of the college in 1925, and he had barely settled in when the chief clerk of the college's Agricultural Experiment Station was discovered to have embezzled upwards of $100,000 in federal funds. The campus was also rocked by an outbreak of venereal disease the following year, and the college surgeon was authorized to charge students ten dollars for "private" treatment (five dollars went to A&M and five dollars to the doctor). The most serious incident of 1926 was the death of A&M student Charles M. Sessums in a riot during an A&M-Baylor football game in Waco. And one of the most telling milestones, perhaps, was the closing of the college zoo, which was located across the railroad tracks from the west campus gate and which had contained an exotic assortment of lions, tigers, snakes, deer, elk, an elephant, and an ostrich.

Although A&M had made a name for itself during the war as a preeminent military school, the ROTC regimen softened a bit during the postwar twenties as student veterans managed to become exempt from the program and as more and more foreign and graduate students enrolled. A number of women also expressed an interest in taking courses at the college, writes Henry C. Dethloff in his centennial history of A&M, and the "old question of admitting women to Texas A&M arose with fresh urgency."[3] Among the gung-ho cadets who had barely missed the fighting in France there was indeed a vicarious sense of fraternity born of

the blood and smoke of Saint-Mihiel and the Argonne Forest, but among others there was less enthusiasm about the martial arts. Now more of a military college than ever, ironically enough, A&M was beginning to attract students who wanted no part of dusty parade grounds and white-glove inspections. The board of directors also continued to investigate the perennial problem of hazing, which became the focus of a statewide public furor in 1924 over the claim (which was to be proved false) that the death of an A&M student was due to his having been forced to drink tobacco juice. According to Dethloff, even "some of the regular students displayed an aversion to the military system."[4]

Academically, A&M emerged from the war with a renewed purpose. Along with its well-earned reputation as a war college came a well-honed specialization in the "practical arts"—engineering, scientific farming, research, the agricultural extension service—which the war had nurtured and which served to reaffirm the college's original reason for being. And alongside its preeminent specialty had grown a department devoted to the art and science of building construction entitled "Architectural Engineering and Drawing," which had been established in 1905 by Frederick E. Giesecke as the state's first formal curriculum in architecture.[5] In the beginning, the curriculum was far more science than art. For freshmen and sophomores, the courses were the same as those of the civil engineering department, and even in the last two years the engineering aspects of building were emphasized over the more ethereal aspects of architectural design. With the organization of the School of Engineering in 1911, architectural engineering became a department therein, and in 1922 the first proposal was

[3] Dethloff, *Centennial History* II, 409.

[4] Ibid.

[5] Ernest Langford, *The First 50 Years of Architectural Education at the Agricultural and Mechanical College of Texas* (College Station: Texas A&M University Archives, 1957), p. 1.

made to establish an autonomous school of architecture as well. By then, although no separate school was in the offing (that wouldn't occur until 1969), the curriculum had become more design oriented, offering a full four-year program in architecture and distinguishing between architecture and architectural engineering, giving seniors the option of specializing in one or the other.

During the department's first decade there was little emphasis on the artistry of architecture, but by World War I the department had adopted an exacting Beaux Arts regimen that put a meticulous emphasis on *design*—how a building is composed, detailed, arranged, rendered, and otherwise made a delight to behold whether it is built or not. Actually, by the time the architecture program at A&M had matured enough to get serious about design, the Beaux Arts approach had already left quite a mark in America. Named for the national art school in Paris, the Ecole des Beaux-Arts (the School of Fine Arts), where it originated in the seventeenth century, Beaux Arts was both a philosophy of design and a method of teaching. It looked upon architecture as a broad urban stroke, replacing the busy individuality of Victorianism with a revival of order and symmetry in everything from the arrangement of grand esplanades and buildings to the placement of neoclassical details thereon. Referring exclusively to the architecture of the past—mainly that of classical Greece and Rome—Beaux Arts emphasized a rigid, scholarly approach to design, and its most important theme was composition: how to combine such architectural elements as proportion, scale, contrast, balance, rhythm, unity, and character into one harmonious whole. A number of Americans attended the school in the middle and late 1800s, and by the time the World's Columbian Exposition was held in Chicago in 1893, the Beaux Arts style had become firmly fixed. Its theories would dominate the education and practice of architecture in America until well into the thirties, when the revolutionary principles of the German Bauhaus and the emerging International Style replaced it with the austere, machinelike architecture of twentieth-century Modernism.

Beaux Arts teaching was done in the *atelier*, or workshop, where instructors and students alike wore cotton or linen smocks, supposedly to guard their clothes against chalk and graphite. As former department head Ernest Langford writes in his history of architectural education at A&M, however, "Its real meaning went deeper than that—it was the trademark of the artist!"[6] In the *atelier*, the student fretted over the infamous *esquisse*, or sketch, which had to be just right or he would be summarily deemed *hors concours*, unfit to compete. Concerned as he had to be with a wide range of problems, the Beaux Arts student worried not only about the *analytique*, or his study of the parts of the building (the classical orders, the colonnade, the pediment, the doorway, the ornament), but also about the arrangement of the *entourage*, or the grounds around it, which could consist of trees, shrubs, grass, walkways, and drives—all of which had to be made into an orderly composition. There was also the archaeology of architecture to consider, as Langford recalled, which was usually done as a research project in which the student with a keen knowledge of architectural history and "who was skilled in composition and rendering really came into his own."[7] As a test of his creative stamina, the *charette* was the final push to complete the *projet*, sometimes running for days at a time and from which the student would emerge "unkempt, unshaven, bleary-eyed." It was a tough and sometimes terrifying approach to architectural education, but it was also effective; by the time a student endured four years of the

[6]Langford, *First 50 Years*, p. 10.
[7]Ibid., p. 11.

atelier, he was fit to compete with just about anybody.

It was into this rigorous academic atmosphere of the bayonet and smock, at about two o'clock on a mid-September morning in 1927, that sixteen-year-old Raiford Stripling, along with three other San Augustine boys (including his buddy Pete Mathews), stepped from the train at College Station with valises in hand. As Mathews remembers, the boys went inside the first building they came to and trudged on up to the second floor. Striking a match to see, they found some steel cots and mattresses, without sheets or pillows, and went fast asleep. "Up early and doing what we were told," Mathews says, they were enrolled in the college by noon and assigned to a 12-by-12-foot room on the second stoop of Leggett Hall, with bunks stacked four high against one wall.

The freshman class entering the department of architecture in the fall of 1927 numbered more than a hundred, and as former design instructor C. A. Johnson recalls, this made it difficult for a faculty of five to provide the kind of personal attention that was best for a course in architectural design. Actually, little architectural design was taught the first year, Johnson says; most of the required courses were academic (chemistry, trigonometry, English, French), except for such basic architectural courses as descriptive geometry and freehand drawing. In spite of this "mob" of freshmen, says Johnson (now in his early eighties and still practicing architecture in Houston), he recognized a "special talent" in the "skinny kid from East Texas," and as attrition took its toll on the class (down to about twenty by the sophomore year), Raiford's talents began to stand out even more. One aspect of the early design courses at which he was particularly adept, says Johnson, was the *analytique*, typically given as the first project the sophomore year and consisting of a collage of historic architectural parts done in

watercolor on a 24-by-36-inch sheet of heavy "double elephant" paper, which was wetted, pasted, stretched, and dried into a painting surface as hard and tight as tanned leather. "He was really quite excellent at that sort of thing," Johnson says.

Raiford did not take so well to the military regimen. In those days, all freshmen ("fish") and sophomores had to belong to the Corps of Cadets. After their second year, students would either be "invited" to continue on in advanced ROTC and perhaps receive a commission as a reserve officer upon graduation or be cut from the program, at which point they would be classified "day students" (or "day ducks") and be allowed to live off campus and attend classes as ordinary college students. It came as no surprise to Raiford, of course, that A&M had more than just a token military way about it—and besides, there was a certain prestige in wearing an army uniform in those days, so soon after World War I, when everyone loved the doughboy. Raiford remembers a next-door neighbor in San Augustine during the war years who had four daughters in their early twenties, "in other words, courtin' age, and the uniforms that would show up there were pretty terrific." To a seven-year-old boy, the sight of a soldier resplendent in jodhpurs, boots, and Sam Browne belt was an impressive one, and ten years later, instead of repelling him, the fact that A&M was a military college made his matriculation there all the more adventurous and romantic.

It didn't take long, however, for the romance to wear off. There are certain aspects of the military that can lose their luster fast, particularly that part of the service that is the essence of soldiering—the infantry—and it was to this somewhat ignoble branch that young Raiford was assigned. For the purist, there is a certain honor in the infantry; less glamorous than the cavalryman and less learned than the artilleryman, the foot soldier is nevertheless the one who

Raiford's Texas A&M cadet company (ca. 1927). Raiford is fourth from the far right, front row.

does the face-to-face "fighting" and most of the medal winning, and calling yourself a soldier without ever having endured the primal discomforts of being in the infantry is like calling yourself a lawyer when you have never argued a case in court or a journalist when you have never written for a daily newspaper. Of course, one drawback that is almost unique to his specialty is the fact that the foot soldier is also the one who does most of the dying, and the preparation for that possibility (or the insurance against it)—the endless route marches and drills, the obstacle courses, becoming one with your rifle, being yelled at by vociferous sergeants—can get old very fast. Assigned to C Company infantry, which was billeted in Leggett Hall, Raiford wasn't too thrilled about it. Although he loved shooting his '03 Springfield on the rifle range, being an officer of foot soldiers was not something he particularly wanted to strive for, and as Raiford went dutifully through the paces, he became less and less the gung-ho volunteer and more and more the recalcitrant draftee.

Not that he was the only student who didn't particularly like being in C Company infantry. In fact, the company as a whole—consisting mostly of East Texas boys from Brenham, Center, Marshall, Diboll, and Nacogdoches—was a rather rowdy group of cadets. To get out of drill, Raiford recalls, they would rub a light cord back and forth across the back of their heels until it created a blister, as though their shoes had caused it, then hobble to the hospital. Pete Mathews recalls one warm night when someone hollered that Capt. Edwin E. "Squirrel-Tooth" Aldridge, a by-the-book infantry officer, was walking around outside the dorm, whereupon five gallons of water was poured out the window and onto the captain's head. "Everyone on the floor was questioned real close," Mathews says, "including 'Strip,' who could always hold a poker face." Then there was "Prexy's Moon," an ordinary bare light bulb that hung from a pipe attached to the dome of the Academic Building. Returning from the range, C Company cadets would always try to pilfer enough ammunition so they could take potshots at the light bulb from the comfort of their own rooms, usually between ten and eleven o'clock at night. (As it happened, the architecture department was on the fourth floor of the Academic Building, Raiford recalls, "so the architectural students were really kinda in range.") Needless to say, there were many demerits issued for shooting at Prexy's Moon, but nothing upset the chain of command quite like the time C Company cadets allegedly destroyed the decorations for the R.V. (Ross Volunteers) Dance in Sbisa Hall. The company was made to fall out in the middle of the night and march to the Brazos River and back, some twenty miles round trip. By then, toward the end of Raiford's sophomore year, C Company infantry had gained such a notorious reputation in the Corps that it was simply disbanded and its troops scattered to various other units. Raiford was also informed by Maj. John E. Sloan, second in command to the commandant, that if his military attitude didn't improve, he would not be recommended for advanced ROTC. As Katy Capt writes in her monograph on Raiford, he was absolutely delighted by the news, and in the fall of 1929 he proceeded with plans to take up residence as a day duck in the Boyett Apartments, a two-story stucco building that still stands on University Avenue just north of campus.[8]

Beaux Arts training had been introduced to A&M by Professor S. J. Fountain, who had studied at the Ecole des Beaux-Arts in Paris and who became head of the department in 1912. When he died in 1914, at the age of thirty-three, "the enthusiasm for the Beaux-Arts system waned for a while," Langford writes, but "began to bud again in the middle and late twenties," reaching "full bloom once more under the direction of S. C. P. Vosper, one of the ablest delineators of modern times."[9]

Samuel Charles Phelps Vosper was born in New Brunswick, New Jersey, on May 19, 1887, the son of John Vosper, an immigrant from Devon County, England, who owned

a shoe factory in New Brunswick, and Frances Thompson Vosper, an amateur painter and watercolorist. He attended Trinity Boy's School in New York City on a scholarship, and in October of 1905, when he was eighteen, Vosper entered the department of architecture at Pratt Institute in Brooklyn. Institute records indicate he was a late registrant (classes started September 25), but he went on to pass all eleven of his courses the first term with high marks. After completing a second term with similar grades, he made it almost completely through a third, withdrawing a month before the term ended. (Partial academic training for the professions was not uncommon in Vosper's day.) After leaving Pratt, he apprenticed with the large New York architecture firm Crow, Lewis, and Wick, working mainly on hospital projects. Meanwhile, his father retired and his parents moved to Arlington, New Jersey, where Vosper, singing in an Episcopal church choir, would meet Augusta Lawrence Westerfield, member of an old New York Dutch-English family. They were married in July of 1914, a union soon stung with grief. Their first child, a son named David, died in infancy after falling from his high chair. But they were soon blessed with a second son, whom they also named David, born in 1917. A year later Vosper was commissioned to help design some lavish real estate development in Florida for the Packard family (of Packard motorcar fame). Hesitant to put too much distance between herself and her ancestral home on Staten Island, at least until she was certain Vosper was ready to settle down somewhere (cross-country travel with a baby was a major effort in those days), Augusta would not accompany him to Florida, which turned out to be a wise decision. Vosper's third son, Bradley, an architect in Amarillo, recalls his father telling him of the ill-fated Florida venture, how after all the excitement of being commissioned by a powerful client to work on a big project, all

[8] Katy Capt, "Raiford Leak Stripling: The Life and Times of an East Texas Restoration Architect" (master's thesis, Texas A&M University, 1981), p. 8.
[9] Langford, *First 50 Years*, p. 9.

Vosper ended up designing was a tea house.

Disappointed in the Packard project, Vosper nevertheless remained in Florida, where he landed a job with a company called "Famous Players," which specialized in designing movie palaces for the burgeoning film industry. It was Famous Players that brought him to Texas for a job around 1920, and Vosper fell in love with the place. After Bradley was born in New York in 1921, Vosper talked Augusta into bringing the baby and joining him in San Antonio, where he went to work as a designer in the office of architect Ralph Cameron. One of Vosper's most notable projects in Cameron's employ was the Medical Arts Building (later called the Landmark Building, now the Emily Morgan Hotel) near the Alamo, a Beaux Arts "Neo-Gothic" high rise with a crenelated cornice and an ornate corner cupola. His other work around the state, all noted for its exquisite detailing and ornamentation, includes the Scottish Rite Cathedral in San Antonio, Shriners' Temple in Dallas, and a number of churches in Dallas and Austin.

According to San Antonio architect Bartlett Cocke, who worked as a young draftsman with Vosper in Cameron's office in 1926, Vosper was a "very peculiar individual." There were six people working for Cameron then, Cocke says, and Cameron kept Vosper in one corner of the office, separated from the rest of the staff. He looked older than he really was, his teeth were bad, and he seemed to "abuse himself," smoking and drinking too much and working a lot at night. And his level of production was somewhat irregular, depending not so much on the volume of work in the office as his own level of inspiration. But when he worked, Cocke says, Vosper was brilliant. He could turn out the most magnificent designs and renderings—and without the kind of brooding, sensitive ego that creative people often have. He laughed a lot—at himself as well as others—and everyone

liked him. "I asked him one time what the S. C. P. stood for in his name," Cocke recalls. "He looked at me in that jolly way of his and said, 'Somewhat Chemically Pure,' then he'd laugh and snort and carry on." Cocke also remembers once when Vosper was designing the Medical Arts Building and drew a beautiful rendering of the project, then signed it "M. O. Frank," who was a young woman fresh out of the University of Texas with a degree in architecture and working in the office as a draftsman. Vosper wasn't exactly a drifter, Cocke says, but he had no talent at all when it came to handling his personal finances and tended to move from one job to another as opportunity arose, "kicking from pillar to post."

One post Vosper kicked in the late twenties was that of a freehand-drawing teacher at the University of Texas at Austin, where it seemed he would finally settle down and raise his family, which by then had grown to include a daughter, Janice, born in San Antonio in 1925. But a happy family life was not to be. Tragedy struck again in 1928, when eleven-year-old David died of blood poisoning from a superficial cut. Although Vosper retained his cheerfully outgoing demeanor, Bradley says, he would never again be as happy-go-lucky as he was before David's death. And although he had always been rather "proper" in a bohemian sort of way, taking pleasure in the finer things in life—good eating, clothing, art, and music—Vosper fought his depression with too much food and drink and grew even more careless about his appearance, his over-six-foot frame gaining more weight than it was designed to carry.

Vosper would be rescued by Frederick Giesecke, a professor in the department of architecture in UT's College of Engineering who recognized Vosper's talents and was sympathetic to his loss. In 1927, after fifteen years at UT, Giesecke returned to A&M to regain the reins as head of the architecture department. (He had been replaced as department head in 1912 by S. J. Fountain.) Giesecke also assumed the responsibilities of college architect, a position that was to become significant as A&M embarked on a campus reconstruction binge paid for by the growing Permanent University Fund. Meanwhile, Vosper, working as a drawing instructor at UT, was substituting live models for the plaster casts then used in the Beaux Arts *atelier*, which, it is said, led to his dismissal and an invitation from Giesecke to come to A&M, where Vosper was made a professor of architecture in September of 1929 and where he would also work as chief designer in the office of the college architect.

September of 1929 was quite an auspicious time in the architecture department at A&M. Along with Vosper came Ernest Langford, who succeeded Giesecke as department head. (Giesecke would continue on as college architect and as director of A&M's Engineering Experiment Station until his retirement.) Langford had actually risen from the ranks at A&M, where he received his degree in architecture in 1913. After a stint in the office of Austin architect A. O. Watson, he returned to A&M as a drawing instructor in 1915, then left again in 1919 for an instructorship at the University of Illinois, where he received his master's degree in 1924. Langford returned to College Station once and for all in 1925, where he would serve twenty-seven years as head of the architecture department and twenty-three years as the mayor of College Station.

Raiford would be influenced by all these men—Johnson, Gilbert "Pop" Giest (a much-loved professor who taught freehand drawing and watercolor), Jack Finney (junior and senior design), Giesecke, and Langford. But no one on the A&M faculty while Raiford was a student there would mold him quite like Samuel Charles Phelps Vosper, who also saw a special talent in Raiford and took it upon himself to foster it.

It didn't take long after his arrival at A&M for Vosper to gain a certain eminence as a beloved campus character as well as a brilliant designer and delineator. He was hard not to notice—a jolly, slovenly bear of a man with delicate hands whom his friends called "Sammy Sunshine." One former student of his remembers Vosper bending over his drawing table giving him a critique, with his head cocked sideways and a cigarette dangling out of one corner of his mouth, its ashes spilling all over the student's rendering. According to Johnson, Vosper seemed much more interested in the "decorative side of architecture than planning' but was "somewhat of a genius in his own way," as well as something of a "bohemian [who] kept odd hours and seemed to do his best work after dark." Raiford remembers Vosper's hands, with their beautifully tapered, blemishless fingers that he didn't bother to keep clean. Raiford also remembers Vosper as a "typical city boy" with an interest in the history of Texas, particularly anything having to do with Sam Houston, and in the vernacular building traditions of the state, especially those of Spanish influence.

In a sense, the relationship that was developing between Vosper and Stripling was like the relationship developing between Dallas architect David Williams and a young neophyte named O'Neil Ford at about the same time. Williams, who was becoming well known for his vernacular style and love for indigenous architecture, took Ford under his wing in 1926, allowing him to sharpen his skills and inclinations as a designer of buildings that were distinctly regional in nature. Like Williams, Vosper (the two were good friends) had a love for local history and building traditions, and like Raiford he had an affinity for the outdoors. Typical city boy that he was, however, Vosper didn't particularly like to hunt, so he would always take along a camera instead of a gun on forays with Raiford to the country to look at old houses and historic sites. As Williams took a slew of photographs of vernacular

Raiford at age twenty.

tograph anything that intrigued his eye. Raiford remembers when Vosper once spent half a day taking pictures of an unusually beautiful cloud formation. "He was just photographing the clouds and sky, you know. He was really an artist, that's what he was."

Under Vosper's artistic tutelage, Raiford came into his own as a designer. During his junior and senior years he produced an award-winning portfolio of Beaux Arts renderings, "the magnificence of which is beyond the imagination of most students of architecture today," writes Katy Capt.[10] Raiford's honors included an award for academic achievement from the American Institute of Architects his junior year and a gold medal in the last annual F. O. Witchell drawing competition his senior year (this competition for A&M architecture students, sponsored by the Dallas firm Lang and Witchell, was discontinued during the depression, and Raiford's gold medal would be stolen by workers during a restoration project later in his career). As a senior, Raiford was also called upon to design the set for the annual Beaux Arts ball as well as a new class ring.

Raiford gained a good bit of practical as well as academic experience during his last years in college, never losing touch with his family or his Deep East Texas roots. Between his junior and senior years he spent the summer in Tyler working for Shirley Simons, architect of the San Augustine County Courthouse. Back in College Station during the school year, Raiford saw a lot of his younger brother Robert, who had been sent to Bryan to finish high school at the Allen Academy, which was a ten-minute trolley ride to the A&M campus. (In 1932, after high school and a couple of years at A&M, Robert too would reject his mother's wish that he become a doctor and instead would go to Washington and work as an aide to East Texas congressman Martin Dies,

structures in Central Texas in the late twenties, so would Vosper survey indigenous architecture with a camera, especially in South Texas. Over the years, Raiford would accumulate (and finally give to A&M) boxes full of black-and-white photographs that Vosper had taken of old houses near San Diego and Roma—pictures of story-and-a-half structures, as Raiford says, all laid in Spanish ashlar with telltale spalls and "an outside stair on one gable or coming off a porch going up to a landing and into the tall end." And as O'Neil Ford's design values were shaped by tours he took, first with an uncle, then with Williams through small towns in Central Texas, so would Raiford's sense of propriety and place be influenced by road trips with Vosper, who would pho-

[10] Capt, "Raiford Leak Stripling," p. 12.

The 1931 Beaux Arts Ball at Texas A&M for which Raiford designed the decorations. Raiford is in the fourth row back, just right of center.

who would establish and serve as chairman of the House Committee on Un-American Activities in 1938. Later, Robert would play a prominent role in the Alger Hiss case, serving as chief investigator for the Un-American Activities Committee and writing a book about it with columnist Bob Considine in 1949.) Raiford also spent a college summer in San Augustine working on a Texaco pipeline crew with several of his A&M buddies, an experience that turned into another test of his mettle and a summer that his brother and sisters would always remember.

As Robert recalls, Texaco had a pumping station a few miles outside of San Augustine that sent oil via pipeline to Port Arthur.

One night the pumps blew up, and overnight San Augustine became a beehive of activity as special task forces from Houston worked around the clock to get the oil flowing again. Texaco recruited local men to dig the ditches for a bypass line in the southern part of the county, and Raiford and some of his huskier friends volunteered. Just as in high school, however, when he first tried out for the baseball team, Raiford had a hard time convincing Texaco that he would make a good laborer. Nevertheless, he eventually talked his way onto the crew, and he worked like a demon all summer with his shirt off, sweating in the sun and turning tan and fit. Deep down, Robert says, Raiford was more proud of making that pipeline crew than of anything he had accomplished. His sister Frances remembers when the boys would come home late on those summer nights, tired and dirty, and what a magnificent sight they were. "We sisters thought they were handsome and delightful and looked from afar at those wonderful Aggies. All we had to do was get out one of Raiford's yearbooks and look at the pictures of the Ross Volunteers and Corps commanders to look past the dirt and grime."

Raiford graduated with a bachelor's degree in architectural design in the spring of 1931, in the very depths of the depression. Although it was a less than opportune time to enter the job market, he did manage to find work immediately with Shirley Simons in Tyler, at ten dollars a week. It is said that he was the only graduate in his class to find a job that year. Even if he hadn't landed the job in Tyler, opportunity was in the offing at A&M. By the fall of 1931, the college was starting to gear up for the campus building program made possible by the Permanent University Fund, and the office of the college architect was getting to be a busy place. Aware that his chief designer and Raiford had become close friends, Giesecke hired Raiford six months after he graduated to return to A&M and assist Vosper. According to Raiford, he was hired mainly to make sure Vosper made it to work in the morning, for Vosper was drinking heavily by now, and sometimes Raiford had to prime him with a couple of shots of whiskey just to get him out of bed.

In April of 1930, the A&M Board of Directors and the UT Board of Regents finally agreed on an equitable division of the Permanent University Fund. For the fiscal year ending August 31, 1931, A&M would receive $150,000, and the same amount for each of three fiscal years thereafter. Then, beginning in September of 1934, A&M would be entitled to one-third of the income from the fund. The agreement also called for the A&M directors and UT regents to re-

quest the legislature to allow money from the fund to be used for capital improvements and not just administration. In April of 1931, the legislature approved a modified bill that allocated $200,000 to A&M for three fiscal years instead of $150,000 for four, marking the beginning of a campus building boom that ironically made the Great Depression a period of unprecedented growth for both schools.

"The impact of this new source of money upon Texas A&M was immediate," writes Henry Dethloff in his centennial history, "and in view of the crucial financial conditions ensuing from the darkening Depression, the results were even spectacular. One is led to wonder if Texas A&M and The University could have survived the Depression without the oil revenues. As it was, both did survive—exceedingly well."[11] Between 1931 and 1933, more than $1.2 million was spent on capital improvements on the A&M campus, including the $167,500 Petroleum Building, the $350,000 Administration Building, the $176,600 Agricultural Engineering Building, the $209,300 Animal Industries Building, and the $132,900 Veterinary Hospital. As Dethloff points out, the A&M campus also underwent a more symbolic change. In July of 1931, A&M deeded to the State Highway Department almost eight acres along the campus's eastern boundary that would serve as the right-of-way for new Texas State Highway 6. The new Administration Building would be built facing the highway, replacing the old Main Building, which faced west and the railroad tracks. "Texas A&M turned away from the railroad and the west," Dethloff writes, "leaving its pioneering days behind, and faced the new highway, the east, and a new era."[12]

Responsible for the master plan and design of the new A&M campus, for the most part, was the office of the college architect,

---

[11] Dethloff, *Centennial History* II, 420.
[12] Ibid., p. 424.

which consisted of some thirty-one employees in 1931, including architects, landscape architects, and structural and mechanical engineers. They were officed in old Ross Hall, a condemned building near the YMCA (where Vosper had an apartment). Giesecke's office was on the first floor, engineers were on the second, and Vosper's office was on the third, where Raiford labored as Vosper's assistant. In addition to making sure Vosper made it to the office in the morning, Raiford also earned his fifty-cents-an-hour wage as a draftsman, along with Leo Norton, "Happy" Padgett, John Astin Perkins, and Elo Urbanovsky, drawing details for Vosper's designs. Although they were limited to that wage for the entire three years Raiford worked there, the draftsmen were not limited to the number of hours they could work. "If we had something coming up that we wanted to have a little money for," Raiford says, "we'd just lay in there with it," sometimes putting in eighty hours a week.

The college architect himself, an engineer by training, was actually more involved with heating the campus buildings than designing them, spending most of his time perfecting his circulating hot-water system, and allowing Vosper to be the real architect of the new campus. Because of his design ability and his friendship with Vosper, Raiford was entrusted with drawing the full-size details of all the ornamental stonework that Vosper specified. Vosper would lay out the details, then Raiford would produce full-size drawings that would go to Italian clay modelers working at a stone plant right on campus, who would create a mold in which to cast the stone. Made from cement and various aggregates, cast stone makes for a somewhat less elegant effect than cut stone, since it isn't hand chiseled and doesn't weather very well. Nevertheless, some of Vosper and Raiford's finest—and most whimsical—details are still very much in evidence

on the Veterinary Hospital (now the Civil Engineering Building), Animal Industries Building, and the Agricultural Engineering Building—everything from horse heads and cow skulls to owls and rats and ears of corn.

When the new Administration Building project came along, Raiford was entrusted with more than just drawing details. Vosper told him he could design the entire west elevation of the building while Vosper designed the more important east elevation. It was an important building as a whole—a monumental Beaux Arts edifice that would present a grand visage to the new and more imposing East Gate. Enhanced by the natural slope of the esplanade that leads up from Highway 6, a long flight of steps leads up to the main entry on the east facade, which is centered in an array of fourteen free-standing Ionic columns. Column capitals, in which Vosper intended to incorporate a stylized portrait of a "typical" A&M cadet, turned out to feature a face that, as Langford writes, looks more like a Greek god sculpted by Phidias. Portending the enrollment of women at A&M, Vosper also included a portrait modeled after Sarah Orth, daughter of the construction superintendent. A detail of the building even more indicative of Vosper's passions is the map of Texas in the floor of the main entrance hall. Within a circle some twelve feet in diameter, set down in brass and terrazzo, is the history of Texas from Spanish colonization to statehood. Among other things, the map indicates the location of missions, battlefields, El Camino Real, and Washington-on-the-Brazos, where the Texas Declaration of Independence was signed in March of 1836.

In addition to helping Vosper detail and design his buildings, Raiford was also charged with accompanying Giesecke when he went to make presentations to the A&M Board of Directors at their meetings in the old Duncan House. Cradling Vosper's beautiful watercolors in his lap, Raiford would sit in the front seat of Giesecke's old Cadillac so he could work the manual gas pump on the dashboard, which someone had to do to keep the gas pressure up and the engine running.

Stripling, Norton, Padgett, Perkins, and Urbanovsky were quite a crew. Working together by day, they also roomed and partied together by night. For a time they all lived in a little log house in College Park, then moved into the very apartment in the Boyett that Raiford had lived in his last two years in school, the center apartment on the bottom floor, which was within walking distance of Ross Hall. The five young bachelor draftsmen played as hard as they worked—largely because they had wheels. Norton's father, a banker in Greenville, furnished his son with a Ford convertible, and every weekend they would drive to dances in Brenham, Calvert, or Navasota. They also paid regular visits to the bootlegger over in Washington County to replenish their ever-dwindling stock of Prohibition booze.

"Raiford was the outstanding graduate in the department of architecture in 1931," says Norton, who first met Raiford in the fall of 1927 when both were freshman architecture students. (Norton would later become a contractor in Dallas.) "He was the most talented one of us all—an artist of exceptional ability." Norton also remembers that Raiford had a wonderful sense of humor and could entertain them for hours telling stories about Deep East Texas. One night in 1931, Norton recalls, when four of them were engaged in a crap game with four young college instructors from a neighboring apartment, Raiford threw the dice and let out with the following: "Teneha, Timpson, Bobo, and Blair skip Bland Lake and make Bogolusy," sounding just like an East Texas sawmill hand (the first five refer to small East Texas towns, the last to Bogalusa, Louisiana). Raiford also was a good dancer, Norton says, and young women al-

ways welcomed him as a partner, including a Bryan girl named Marjorie Cavitt, whom Raiford dated at A&M and would meet and date again years later.

Along with all four of his fellow draftsmen—as well as his mentor Vosper—Raiford could put away his share of bootleg liquor, which became a source of concern to some of the people who thought he had an unlimited future in architecture. Although Norton says he always carried it well, others, such as C. A. Johnson, Raiford's freshman and sophomore drawing instructor, thought some of Vosper's worst habits were starting to rub off on his protégé. When Johnson would see Raiford and his pals on campus in the early thirties, he would always be surprised and disappointed in Raiford's appearance. "He had gotten thinner, if that were possible," Johnson says. "I don't consider myself a prude, having imbibed a little 'Washington County Corn' in my time, but I felt that Raiford and his group seemed to be overdoing it a bit." Raiford himself recognized Vosper's propensity to overindulge, but drinking whiskey contributed as much to the manly camaraderie of Raiford's team of young draftsmen as it did to Vosper's chronic inability to rise and shine. In his early twenties, Raiford was indeed forming lifelong habits that would later haunt him, and Vosper's influence was not all positive, but Raiford could handle himself. "Yeh, Vosper hit the booze real good," he says. "That's something else he and I agreed on. He'd always have something to drink, and I could keep up with him. Then I'd drink him under the table, 'cause he'd get drunk and I wouldn't."

By the winter of 1933, the Great Depression finally visited A&M. Although oil royalties continued to flow into the Permanent University Fund, the effects of the stock-market crash, bank failures, and dwindling college enrollments across the country forced A&M to tighten its belt like everybody else. Staff salaries were reduced, positions eliminated, and departments merged. As the office of the college architect came off its warlike footing, Vosper began looking for another place to exercise his and Raiford's talents. The first opportunity to present itself was a job with the depression-spawned Civil Works Administration (CWA) in San Antonio, where Vosper and Raiford moved in the fall of 1933 to live in an old Spanish house and to design city park facilities—bathhouses, shelters, and the like. Raiford even spent a month down in Laredo laying out a golf course. After about seven months in San Antonio, Raiford and Vosper were both transferred to the CWA office in Austin, where Raiford would work for a short while with fellow CWA architect O'Neil Ford.

Also in Austin, as it happened, the University of Texas was still building a new campus financed by its larger share of the Permanent University Fund and according to the inspired designs of Philadelphian Paul Cret, a Beaux Arts architect of national renown. Cret was working closely with UT's supervising architect Robert Leon White, whom Vosper had known when he was a drawing instructor there, and Vosper was able to get Raiford a job in White's office drawing details for Cret's designs. Working for Cret not only presented a chance for Raiford to be gainfully employed, but it was also a golden opportunity for him to learn from yet another master designer. So in the fall of 1934, as Vosper took a job with the National Park Service—which was spearheading a new movement to save historic buildings across the country by putting unemployed architects, historians, and craftsmen back to work—Raiford went to work for UT's "college architect." There, after seven years in College Station, he was to further refine his hand and eye and prepare for a new field of architecture that seemed tailor-made for this skinny kid from historic San Augustine and one that he would embrace with a passion.

CHAPTER 4

Prospects

Before 1926 the thought of taking an old, weather-beaten building and spending thousands of dollars fixing it up just so people could appreciate its "historical" value would have seemed ludicrous to most Americans. Progressive thinkers in the 1920s, like San Augustine County Judge Raif Stripling, were growing infatuated with the prospects of Modernism, which would soon be manifested in a variety of forms—not the least among them architecture. Replacing the ideas and techniques of the backward-looking Beaux Arts were the revolutionary notions of the Bauhaus, a school of architecture and related arts and crafts founded by architect Walter Gropius in 1919 in Weimar, Germany. Like the Beaux Arts, the Bauhaus was both philosophy and method. Unlike the Beaux Arts, the Bauhaus rejected any allusion to the past for inspiration, turning instead to the magnificence of the Machine Age.

Already celebrating the iron and mechanical workings of the Industrial Revolution were such wonders as the Crystal Palace in London, designed by Sir Joseph Paxton and built in 1851, and the Eiffel Tower in Paris, designed by Gustave Eiffel for the Paris International Exhibition of 1889. Meanwhile, architects of the Chicago school—Louis Sullivan and Holabird and Roche, among others—were developing the steel-frame skyscraper, and Frank Lloyd Wright was creating his "organic architecture," which—particularly in his residential designs—hugged the earth like no other kind of architecture had before. Before being closed by the Nazis in 1933, the Bauhaus (which was moved in 1925 to Dessau and in 1932 to Berlin) employed an illustrious faculty, including Hungarian architect Marcel Breuer and German architect Ludwig Mies van der Rohe, both of whom would flee Hitler's Germany in the late 1930s (along with Gropius) and spread the teachings of the Bauhaus at schools of architecture in the United States. And the Modern architecture of Swiss-born French architect Charles Edouard Jeanneret, known as Le Corbusier, as well as that of Mies, Gropius, and others, would become known as the International Style, thanks to a book and exhibition by that name published and staged in 1932 by American architectural historian Henry-Russell Hitchcock and Philip Johnson, then director of the department of architecture at the Museum of Modern Art in New York.

There is no small irony in the fact that, just as the Modern movement in architecture was taking hold in the late twenties and early thirties, replacing the eclectic, classical-revival styles of the past, the Great

Depression would focus national attention on America's architectural heritage, and the federal government would hire thousands of architects to record and preserve it. The reasons for this interest in the past were not entirely economic. In addition to sleek lines and smooth surfaces, Modernism also meant drive-ins, gas stations, motels, billboards, and all the other commercial trappings of the most ubiquitous machine of all—the automobile. While giving American tourists the unprecedented mobility to drive around and see historic sites, the car also created the cluttered commercial strip, which began to violate the historic purity of those sites, including the old tidewater town of Williamsburg, Virginia. Although the settlement had already lost much of its colonial charm, there were enough pieces left to interest John D. Rockefeller, Jr., who agreed to finance the town's restoration. Beginning in 1926, three years before Black Tuesday, the project soon turned into the largest and most exhaustive restoration of its kind, involving the destruction or relocation of more than 450 "modern" buildings and the reconstruction and restoration of some 150 buildings to the way they were before 1775.

Before Colonial Williamsburg, historic preservation had been mainly a private, piecemeal affair. A few notable projects had been undertaken, such as the restoration of Mount Vernon by the Mount Vernon Ladies' Association, begun in 1859. And discourse among architectural thinkers had already raised some significant issues about the saving of old buildings. Critic John Ruskin and architect William Morris, both Englishmen who greatly influenced architectural thought in America in the nineteenth century, spoke out against the kind of restoration practiced by French architect Viollet-le-Duc. Whereas Viollet-le-Duc thought nothing of ripping away any elaboration on a building's original form to return it to a certain period, Ruskin and Morris felt that to "restore" a building in such a way was to

destroy it. Before Williamsburg, there was also a little national legislation, such as the Antiquities Act of 1906, which authorized the president of the United States to designate "National Monuments" wherever there were structures of historic significance on public lands. And the War Department administered a number of Civil War battlefields and Indian ruins across the country. But the Williamsburg restoration marked the first time that a preservation effort had been undertaken on such a scale and with such organization. Legions of architects, historians, archaeologists, landscape architects, draftsmen, craftsmen, contractors, and laborers were assembled to learn about historic preservation on the job. By 1928, as Charles B. Hosmer, Jr., points out in his history of preservation in America, the Williamsburg project had become the "first school of architectural restoration in the United States," and the one professional who emerged as the leader of this monumental effort was the architect, who was the only specialist of the lot in the 1920s who was already "history-minded." Even the historian "merely paid lip service to the idea that buildings could be classed as documents."[1] Unveiled in 1934, the Williamsburg restoration served as the perfect testing and training ground for historic preservation in America as the depression transformed it from an amateurish, ad hoc effort to a concerted, scholarly movement—with the architect leading the way.

Progress on most other fronts came to a halt in 1929. Even visionaries like Judge Stripling, who had been "just about wiped out in the panic of 1929 and forced to sell all his cattle and much of his land," according to his youngest son Robert, were beginning to have second thoughts about the beneficence of the Modern Age. As unemploy-

[1] Charles B. Hosmer, Jr., *Preservation Comes of Age: From Williamsburg to the National Trust, 1926–1949* (Charlottesville: University Press of Virginia, 1981), I, 31.

ment spread, the last thing many architects practicing outside New York, Chicago, or academe were thinking about was the latest theoretical precepts of their trade; although the International Style represented one of the most dramatic departures from the architectural norm that the world had ever witnessed, most architects were more concerned about getting food on the table than they were about following any fascinating trends. And by 1933, opportunity for unemployed designers and draftsmen came largely in the form of New Deal recovery programs affiliated with the National Park Service, which had been charged with, among other things, administering the newly established Historic American Buildings Survey (HABS).

Organized in 1916 as a branch of the Department of the Interior, the National Park Service had been responsible for maintaining a number of designated National Monuments in the Southwest as "historical exhibits." Like the War Department, however, the Park Service had no real professional staff to interpret and effectively administer these sites. Then in 1931 Verne E. Chatelain was hired as official park historian, and the Park Service gained a certain credibility as well as a staunch advocate of historic preservation. Remembering his boyhood in a part of Nebraska that Lewis and Clark had explored, as Charles Hosmer writes, Chatelain once said he appreciated then "how important the physical site is to the effective realization of historical conditions and events."[2] In 1933, due largely to the efforts of Park Service director Horace Albright, all historical parks were transferred from the War Department to the Department of the Interior, and Albright proceeded to "go rather heavily into the historical park field."[3]

This new direction for the Park Service was facilitated by the creation of the Civilian Conservation Corps (CCC), which was intended to put some two hundred thousand unemployed youth from the cities to work in American parks and forests by mid-June 1933. Then in November, HABS was proposed to employ some one thousand CWA architects to make measured drawings of vernacular structures (houses, forts, stores, outbuildings, mills) built before 1850 and in danger of being demolished. The purpose of HABS was not to save these structures but to record them for posterity—and, above all, to put unemployed architects and draftsmen back to work. Administered by the Park Service, the program was conducted in cooperation with the American Institute of Architects (AIA), which, through its local chapters, furnished the field inspectors who selected the buildings to be surveyed, and with the Library of Congress, which provided the archival facilities.

Given a definite boost by these New Deal programs, the Park Service's involvement in historic preservation during the early days of the depression was still rather inconsistent. Much depended on federal funding, which could be somewhat irregular, and on local politics and priorities, which understandably placed more emphasis on needy people than on needy buildings. And it soon became clear that the only legislation on the books that specifically addressed historic preservation—the Antiquities Act of 1906—was inadequate for dealing with the somewhat disjointed make-work crusade that the preservation movement was fast becoming. In short, there was still no permanent, broad-based policy regarding historic preservation—no official program like that of the Office of Works in Great Britain, the Commission des monuments historiques in France, or the Soprintendenza dei monumenti in Italy—that went beyond the economic exigencies of the day. Williamsburg was a good model, but it was still a local, private phenomenon. What the United States needed was a law that would consoli-

[2] Ibid., p. 514.
[3] Ibid., p. 476.

date the effort on the national level and provide for the orderly designation, acquisition, and preservation of properties deemed worthy of salvation.

Then in August 1935, Roosevelt signed the Historic Sites Act, which had been sponsored in the House by first-term Texas congressman Maury Maverick of San Antonio. Although not a legislative panacea for all that ailed the movement, the act did establish guidelines and mechanisms for preserving historically significant buildings. Among other things, it called for a nationwide survey of historic sites, cooperation between the public and private sectors in their maintenance, and the formation of an advisory board to assist the secretary of the interior in putting together a national network of historic parks, buildings, and monuments.

Problems the act failed to address were more philosophical in nature. As the methods of historic preservation became more and more refined, conflict began to emerge not so much over *how* to preserve as *what* to preserve. Architectural historian Henry-Russell Hitchcock argued that some of the most architecturally significant buildings of the nineteenth century—especially those of the late Victorian period—were being ignored, while most of the preservation emphasis was being placed on pre-Revolutionary buildings for the sake of "patriotic education." The movement was also biased toward preserving the grand architecture of the ruling elite—mansions, statehouses, and the like—at the expense of the humble vernacular houses and shops that have always made up most of the built environment. Although this ordinary "folk architecture" was being systematically documented by HABS, it wasn't being systematically preserved. Questions inevitably arose: Just what does "historical" or "architectural significance" mean? Does a building have to be grand to be exemplary? Is a building worthy of preservation just by virtue of having had some-

thing historic happen inside of it, whether it represents an important period of American architecture or not? Is a building worthy of preservation just because it's old?

Nowhere would these questions arise more intensely than in San Antonio in the late thirties, where Congressman Maverick, co-sponsor of the Historic Sites Act and newly elected mayor of San Antonio, campaigned to designate the old Mexican settlement of La Villita by the river in downtown San Antonio as a National Historic Site. In spite of the help of young San Antonio architect O'Neil Ford in restoring the village, using labor and funds from the National Youth Administration (NYA), La Villita was considered by Park Service historians to be a somewhat undistinguished—albeit old—assortment of structures, and it would fail to gain any official federal designation until 1972. When it comes to old buildings, as Hitchcock and Maverick were well aware, "significance" is an ever-changing value. Unappreciated in the 1930s by even the most well-intentioned, Victorian architecture is now the beloved recipient of a great deal of preservation money and expertise, and today La Villita sits proudly on the National Register of Historic Places, a showcase on San Antonio's famed Paseo del Rio. (The River Walk itself, which began as a beautification and flood-control plan in the late twenties, was conceived by San Antonio architect Robert H. H. Hugman, who designed and supervised the development as a Works Progress Administration [WPA] project in the late thirties.)

Questions of how far to go in the preservation of a building in the 1930s also involved a new set of definitions. There was the scholarly "house-museum" approach, which involved "restoring" a building to a certain historic point in time, resulting in a pristine work of architecture to look at but not touch; there was the "reconstruction" of a building that no longer exists, which involved even more research and educated guesswork; then there was simple "preservation," which was intended to repair and maintain the building as is. (Not yet popular in the 1930s were a number of other levels of historic preservation, such as "adaptive reuse," which would involve restoring an old building's exterior while modernizing its interior for new purposes.)

In spite of raising almost as many questions about the protection of old architecture as it answered, there is no question that the depression institutionalized historic preservation in the United States. Economic collapse caused a kind of nostalgic reappreciation of America's past, and New Deal recovery programs provided the manpower and money to explore it. In the process, a whole generation of architects, historians, and archaeologists fresh out of universities in the late 1920s and early 1930s came to constitute a cadre of professional preservationists who would lead the movement to even better days.

Although he didn't realize it as he made his way to Austin in 1934, young Raiford Stripling was soon to become a leader of that cadre's Texas contingent. So much was pointing Raiford in that direction as it was that he probably couldn't have avoided becoming a preservation architect even if he had wanted to; his particular specialization in architecture seemed downright preordained. Raiford was born and reared in one of the most historic towns in the state; he was trained as a Beaux Arts designer steeped in historicism, graduating with a degree in architecture just as the preservation movement got under way; he had a natural, almost romantic interest in the dramatic history of Texas; and he would become a licensed architect about the time the state celebrated its centennial, which was the first statewide promotion of historic preservation in Texas.

Meanwhile, Raiford continued to hone his skills as a draftsman. During the year and a half he spent in Austin in the office of

UT's supervising architect, in the old YMCA building, Raiford's major responsibility was drawing details for Cret's design of the UT Tower, which would contain the stacks of the new library and be the centerpiece of the new UT campus. Throughout his tenure there, Raiford would be as much in awe of Cret's abilities as he was of Vosper's. "Cret was sharp," Raiford says. "He was just like old man Vosper. He could pick up a pencil and make it talk."

The UT Board of Regents hired Paul Philippe Cret, a French-born architect trained at the Ecole des Beaux-Arts in Paris, as consulting architect in March of 1930. He was the second consulting architect of national prominence to design buildings for UT; the first, New York architect Cass Gilbert, whose exquisite library (now Battle Hall) established a Spanish-Mediterranean style for the UT campus when it was built in 1911, served as consulting architect from 1910 to 1922. From then until Cret was appointed, other buildings constructed on campus—most of which were designed by Dallas architect Herbert M. Greene (later the firm Greene, LaRoche, and Dahl)—conformed to this Spanish-Mediterranean style. Appointed supervising architect in 1924, Robert Leon White argued for an even more regionally appropriate style for the UT campus: a Spanish Colonial Revival style with roots in the eighteenth-century Spanish colonial architecture of the Southwest. (Spanish Colonial Revival was a fashionable style in the late teens and throughout the twenties in Southern California, Florida, and Texas, where it was particularly popular in the Rio Grande Valley during a real estate boom in the late twenties, based less on regional building traditions than on a romantic imagery that came across well in promotional brochures.) White had researched the eighteenth-century mission San José y San Miguel de Aguayo in San Antonio when he practiced there in the early twenties, and in the process he had developed a keen interest in Spanish colonial architecture. And it was White who recommended Cret, whose associate architect on his most famous work, the Pan American Union Building in Washington, D.C. (1907), had been fellow Philadelphian Albert Kelsey, who designed the University Baptist Church in Austin (1921) in the Spanish Colonial Revival Style.

Commissioned in 1930 to lay out a new master plan for UT as well as design new buildings, Cret positioned his monumental new library as the heart of campus, replacing the Victorian Gothic Old Main Building (1899), designed by Frederick E. Ruffini. Fortunately for Cret, the state legislature apportioned the Permanent University Fund in April of 1931, and in June of that year the Board of Regents borrowed $4 million against UT's two-thirds share of it for ten new buildings, including the new library, which would be built in stages as additional money became available (the project would also receive a loan from the Public Works Administration in 1933). The thirty-two-story tower, completed in 1937 and reminiscent of Bertram Goodhue's capitol building in Lincoln, Nebraska (1932), not only provided a distinctive architectural symbol for the new UT campus but also served as the skyline counterpoint to the capitol of Texas (1888) some ten blocks to the south, both of which would dominate the Austin skyline for years. The top of the tower was designed to be viewed from afar as a glittering crown, featuring an intricacy of columns, scrolls, moldings, plinths, shells, clock faces, and broken pediments—all of which Raiford painstakingly drew as part of the working drawings that White's office prepared for the project. (Years later, in the summer of 1966, when attention was indeed drawn to the top of the tower while Charles Whitman used it as a sniper's perch, Raiford was in Austin restoring the French Legation [see chapter 6]. As Whitman ran around the tower's observation deck, shooting people on the ground and dodging return fire from police helicop-

ters hovering overhead, Raiford watched from the Legation on a hill to the east while ambulances rushed the wounded to Brackenridge Hospital. "Of course," he told Katy Capt, "I didn't get anywhere close to it, but I had detailed all of that thing, so I knew ever' stone he was hiding behind up there on that tower.")[4]

Although separated by distance and duty, Raiford did not lose touch with Samuel Charles Phelps Vosper. One day his beloved—if somewhat insolvent—mentor walked into White's office, where most of the staff had been students of Vosper's at one time or another, and passed his hat to help pay for a trip to the Big Bend. The Park Service had assigned Vosper to paint a series of watercolors of the area, which had been nominated to become a national park, and Vosper didn't have enough money to get there. So his former students pitched in thirty-five dollars and Raiford and a fellow draftsman took the money to a bookie's office in the Norwood Building downtown and bet it on a horse named Dr. Perkins, which was running that day at Alamo Downs in San Antonio. Dr. Perkins won, paying about ten to one, and Vosper wound up with more than three hundred dollars to travel to Big Bend and back. Raiford says he got such a kick out of financing Vosper's trip with "racehoss money" that the first bird-dog puppy he got after that he named Dr. Perkins, "and he was a good dog."

Raiford left White's office in the spring of 1935 to join Vosper in Goliad and establish a firm for the practice of architecture. Although they had been pupil and teacher, protégé and mentor for seven years, and had even collaborated on a "school or two" in East Texas, this was the first time they practiced together as bona fide partners. And there was plenty to keep them busy in

[4] Katy Capt, "Raiford Leak Stripling: The Life and Times of an East Texas Restoration Architect" (master's thesis, Texas A&M University, 1981), p. 28.

Goliad. Well aware of Vosper's interest in the Spanish missions, the National Park Service drew him to Goliad in the first place with the commission to restore Mission Espíritu Santo, but there was a wealth of design work to be had as the state of Texas, the Park Service, and the Goliad State Park Commission geared up for the Texas centennial in 1936. In addition to Espíritu Santo, Vosper and Stripling, Architects, with offices in the front room of a rented house half a block from the courthouse square (they slept in the back), was commissioned to design the Goliad Memorial Auditorium and the Fannin Battlefield Memorial.

In the winter of 1935, not long after his arrival in Goliad, Raiford was charged with a preservation project of his own—the reconstruction of Fort Parker near Mexia. Park Service historian Bill Hogan had seen the working drawings for Espíritu Santo that Raiford had prepared and thought he could do a good job of designing a replica of the compound, which had been established in 1834 as a private fort near the headwaters of the Navasota River to protect a settlement of nine frontier families. On May 19, 1836, less than a month after the Battle of San Jacinto, hundreds of Comanche and Caddo Indians raided the fort, killed several of its founders, and made off with a handful of women and children, including nine-year-old Cynthia Ann Parker and her six-year-old brother John. In captivity, Cynthia Ann would become the wife of Comanche chief Peta Nocona, and their son Quanah would be the last Comanche chief. In 1860, at the battle of Pease River, Texas Ranger captain Lawrence Sullivan Ross captured Cynthia Ann and her baby Prairie Flower, both of whom lie buried alongside Quanah at Fort Sill, Oklahoma. Considering all that of sufficient historical import, the Commission of Control for Texas Centennial Celebrations allocated $10,000 in 1936 to build a replica of the fort and a caretaker's house on the original one-acre site, which was part of a 1,496-acre plot

donated to the state by the city of Mexia and the citizens of Mexia and Groesbeck.

The Commission of Control for Texas Centennial Celebrations had been organized in May of 1935 to approve plans and appropriate money for "celebrations" across the state to commemorate the Texas centennial. These celebrations included the placing of historic markers and monuments; the staging of "pageants"; and "the restoring of all or parts of old houses, forts, Indian villages, and other old structures connected with the history of the territory now embraced within the State of Texas."[5] Projects were recommended by the three-member Advisory Board of Texas Historians (including J. Frank Dobie), which investigated their historical merit and authenticity. Although the Texas Central Centennial Exposition in Dallas would get most of the fanfare—with its world's-fair scale, Art Deco architecture, grand esplanades, and searchlights sweeping the sky (and Paul Cret as consulting architect)—a good deal of money and effort went into the smaller provincial celebrations that were held throughout 1936, which usually revolved around some kind of historical theme. With the federal government by then a well-oiled machine when it came to historic preservation and public works, Texas couldn't have celebrated its centennial at a better time. A United States Centennial Commission had been appointed in June of 1935 to oversee $3 million in appropriations for the Texas centennial, which state and federal officials viewed as a wonderful opportunity to create jobs and promote tourism. In addition, the Public Works Administration (PWA) and the WPA provided a total of $1,160,000 in grants for various centennial projects around the state. Using CCC labor and working with Park Service architect J. F. Denning and re-

---

[5] *Monuments Commemorating the Centennial of Texas Independence: The Report of the Commission of Control for Texas Centennial Celebrations* (Austin, 1938), p. 9.

search historian Bill Hogan, Raiford designed a replica of Fort Parker, basing his reconstruction on the location of postholes, fireplaces, and stone foundations, and on whatever Hogan could find out about the fort, and specifying cedar timbers for the palisade stockade. The project also included two blockhouses, six cabins, plumbing, water and electrical systems, and display cases for relics found on the site.

Back in Goliad, Raiford continued to work on Espíritu Santo, an assignment somewhat more meaningful in terms of Texas history and, as it would turn out, much more meaningful in terms of Raiford's personal as well as professional life.

There is no question about the historical significance of the Goliad missions. The Spanish mission Nuestra Señora del Espíritu Santo de Zuñiga and its protective fort, Presidio La Bahía, were built on either side of the San Antonio River at what is now Goliad, some ninety miles southeast of San Antonio, in 1749. They were part of a system of presidio-missions established on the Spanish frontier in Florida and from Texas to California, beginning in the late sixteenth century. In Texas this Spanish effort began in response to the wanderings of French explorer René Robert Cavelier, Sieur de La Salle, who landed at Matagorda Bay by mistake in 1685 while looking for the mouth of the Mississippi and who established a short-lived French colony nearby on Garcitas Creek. Intended to civilize and Christianize the native Indians as well as mark the territory for Spain, the presidio-mission strategy was not a particularly successful one, even though it had worked well in Mexico. It was based on a kind of imperialistic, church-state formula that sent forth "the Cross with the Crown": first came the conquistador to subjugate the savages; next, the *encomendero* to set up an economic system; then the padre, to establish the mission and civilize and convert the Indians. That done, the idea was to absorb the Indians into Span-

ish society, distribute the mission lands among them, and for the padres to move on. The whole process was supposed to take about ten years.

Unfortunately, things didn't quite work out that way. Not only were the Indians in Texas less civilized than the Indians in Mexico and less than amenable to Spanish designs, but even those who were seemed to suffer for their cooperation. Whole tribes of coastal Indians were wiped out with "European" diseases—measles, cholera, smallpox. And after the horse was introduced to the Plains Indians, who proved remarkably adept at mounted warfare, the Spanish (and later the Mexicans and Anglos) would live in a heightened state of peril. Mexico finally overthrew Spanish rule in 1821, and by 1830 all Texas missions had been secularized, something Spain had wanted to achieve since 1793, when she decided to cut her losses in the New World. As more and more land-grant immigrants and frontiersmen moved into Texas from the United States, things got progressively worse. Anglo colonies established on the coastal plain between the Colorado and the Brazos by empresarios like Stephen F. Austin and Green DeWitt, sanctioned by the Mexican government as buffers against the Indian presence, served only to aggravate an inherently strained relationship between Mexicans and Texans. Nominally charged with loyalty to the Mexican government, Anglo settlers could exercise such loyalty only to the extent that they could be left well enough alone. Cultural prejudices on both sides and attempts by the Mexican government to clamp down on Anglo colonization made the relationship even worse, and in September of 1835 Austin issued a call to the Texas colonists to take up arms against Mexico.

By December of 1835, the ragtag Texan army held the two most strategically important fortresses on the southern flank of Anglo Texas—the Alamo in San Antonio and La Bahía in Goliad, both former Spanish presidios now turned against Mexico. Following the fall of the Alamo in March of 1836, attention shifted to Goliad, where Col. James W. Fannin commanded a force of five hundred raw recruits, many of whom were Georgia volunteers. Retreating deeper into Anglo Texas and hoping to recruit more men along the way, Gen. Sam Houston ordered Fannin to blow up the presidio and join in his tactical withdrawal. For whatever reason, Fannin—who had been hell-bent on using his force to invade Matamoros—ignored Houston's order, choosing instead to dispatch one-third of the force to aid in the evacuation of nearby Refugio, where it was decimated by approaching Mexican troops under the command of Gen. José Urrea.

Fannin had already developed a reputation for poor military judgment. Upon taking command of the garrison at Goliad in January, he had chosen to use his men as laborers in fortifying the presidio, even though they were in dire need of all the military training they could get. The work was done according to the plans of Fannin's adjutant, Capt. Joseph M. Chadwick of Exeter, New Hampshire, who supervised the men in strengthening the stone walls of the presidio and rebuilding the corner bastions. According to one account, a trenchlike walkway was also built from the northwest corner of the fort down to the river, about two hundred yards away, so that defenders could have secure access to water.

Before Fannin's improvement of the presidio could be completed, he received an urgent plea from Col. William Travis to come to his aid in defense of the Alamo. Setting out from "Fort Defiance" (as Fannin had renamed La Bahía) with three hundred men and four cannon, Fannin soon realized he was pitifully unprepared for such an expedition. He and his troops had gone no farther than the river when one of the wagons broke down, making it difficult to get the artillery across. They also lacked the provisions to make it all the way to San Antonio, and they were fearful of leaving Fort Defiance undermanned and vulnerable to attack. Camping for the night on the other side of the river, Fannin and his officers decided to turn back.

Only after receiving word from a scout that a large enemy force was nearing Fort Defiance, five days after Houston's order to evacuate, did Fannin prepare to leave. After burying cannon, burning foodstuffs, and destroying the fortifications of the presidio, Fannin and his men headed northeast to Victoria, which lay across some twenty-five miles of prairie. Slowed by the weight of cannon and overloaded carts, the procession stopped to rest in an open field near Coleto Creek, where they were overwhelmed by Urrea's superior force. Fannin surrendered in good faith, assuming he and his men would be treated honorably as prisoners of war, but that was not to be. Much to Urrea's resistance, Mexico's President Antonio López de Santa Anna insisted that Urrea follow the high command's standing order that all Texans captured under arms be executed. Urrea did not attend the executions (historians are unsure of exactly why), so the responsibility fell to one Col. José Nicolás de la Portilla. Ambulatory prisoners were marched back to Goliad, the more seriously wounded carried in carts, all believing they would eventually be sent by ship to New Orleans after pledging never to take up arms against Mexico again. The prisoners were first crammed into the presidio chapel, then as their ranks grew to more than four hundred with the addition of prisoners from the Refugio rescue force, they were moved to the west side of the compound. Finally, on Palm Sunday, March 27, 1836, prisoners were marched out of the fort in three columns under heavy guard, believing they were going to Copano, the closest seaport. Less than a mile from Fort Defiance, on three separate roads, the prisoners were shot, as were the wounded who were kept behind at the presidio, including Colonel Fannin. The bodies of some 340 Texans were then thrown into three big piles and burned, their charred remains left exposed to the buzzards and coyotes. After word of the massacre reached Houston and his men, their decisive victory at San Jacinto in April ending the Texas War for independence was studded with the battle cry, "Remember the Alamo, Remember Goliad!" Finally, on June 3, victorious Texans under the command of Gen. Thomas J. Rusk buried the bones of Fannin and his men with full military honors. Texas historians have theorized that, had Santa Anna allowed the prisoners to be shipped to New Orleans, he would have scored an invaluable publicity coup: the men would have returned with tales of disunity and indecisiveness on the part of the Texan command, which could have weakened U.S. support for the Texas cause. As it was, writes T. R. Fehrenbach in his history of Texas and the Texans, "Santa Anna made 400 martyrs, and even immortalized James Fannin."[6]

The mission at Goliad had certainly escaped the limelight of history that had fallen upon the presidio, but it was a historically significant assortment of structures in its own right. It was originally built of timber in 1722 in what is now Jackson County, named in part for Baltasar de Zuñiga, then the viceroy of Spain. The presidio, Nuestra Señora de Loreto, was built two miles away at the site of La Salle's French colony on Garcitas Creek. In 1726, the mission and its presidio were moved to the southwest, to what is now Victoria County, to a site on the Guadalupe River just north of Victoria that is still marked by the remains of its stone walls, dam, and acequia system. Finally, in 1749, the mission-presidio complex was moved to Goliad and everlasting glory.

[6]T. R. Fehrenbach, *Lone Star: A History of Texas and the Texans* (New York: American Legacy Press, 1978), p. 227.

Although the presidio served a vital function in providing a military presence for the region, the mission represented the noblest cause of Spanish colonialism: bringing civilization to the Indians. And no small part of that missionary effort, in addition to inculcating the values of Christianity and modern agricultural practices (including the art of herding cattle on horseback), was the architecture of the mission itself. Usually designed to be a temporary structure, a mission was inevitably improved upon once it had been in one place long enough and once its Indian "neophytes" had become proficient enough at the building trades to make it a Spanish Baroque beacon in the wilderness—as close to the extravagance of the Baroque style as conditions on the frontier would permit.

The Texas missions, considered closer to the Spanish Baroque than any of the missions in the colonial Southwest, were embellished according to ecclesiastical styles imported from Spain and filtered through the designs of Franciscan friars from missionary colleges in Zacatecas and Querétaro, Mexico, who were in charge of setting up and administering the missions. The most distinctive carryover from the Old World to the New was the Moorish influence on Spanish architecture—luxurious ornament, carved stone, polychromatic tile, graceful arches, and domes. Primitively alluding to the styles of the day, missions in Texas were eventually built of soft, easily carved limestone laid in mortar made of lime and sand, which formed thick walls with few openings. Fired in mission kilns, brick and tile were sometimes used for floors and moldings. And whatever wood was available in the area—oak, cypress, pecan, cedar, mesquite—was made into lintels, doors, beams, choir lofts, altars, confessionals, pulpits, and furniture. Buildings within the mission complex, along with the stockade walls, were arranged to form an enclosed compound, although the "mission" would often grow outside its walls to encompass whole communities and thousands of acres of ranchland. The most important building, the mission church or presidio chapel, was generally basilican or cruciform in plan, with a facade featuring one or two belfry towers, a rounded central gable, and intricately carved ornamentation around the main entrance. Church roofs were usually masonry domes or barrel vaults, while lesser structures were topped with low-pitched wooden roofs.

And just as Spanish settlements were laid out according to certain proportional systems, so were many of the Spanish missions. Studies have shown that three of the mission churches in San Antonio were designed according to a system of geometric proportions based on the square, the circle, and the eight-pointed star. Building codes also called for windows and doors to be aligned to take advantage of prevailing breezes, and the thick masonry walls provided coolness and shade as well as security. The constraints and qualities of climate, materials, and workmanship shaped this Spanish Baroque architecture in a way that is wholly appropriate to its setting and, as UT architecture dean Hal Box writes, "in a way that is extremely satisfying to Texans."[7]

Not quite as distinctive as some of the missions in San Antonio, Espíritu Santo in Goliad was nevertheless a finely crafted complex. It was originally little more than a chapel of *jacal* or *palisado* construction, as most structures in South Texas were in those days. Poles cut from the surrounding scrub brush would be tied together horizontally or vertically to form the walls, which would be topped with a hipped roof of pole rafters covered with straw, palmetto, caliche, mud, and assorted other earthen ingredients. By 1758 the mission was made of limestone and mortar and consisted of a church, friary, re-

fectory, kitchen, offices, cells, and missionary houses. The church roof was typically barrel vaulted, with a corner belfry tower hexagonal in plan and containing an unsupported spiral staircase made of hand-hewn logs. Indians lived in *jacal* houses around the perimeter.

In 1754 problems among the various tribes in the area led the Franciscans to build a separate mission for the Cujane Indians about five miles west of the presidio, on the banks of the San Antonio River. Mission Nuestra Señora del Rosario, according to some accounts, was originally more finely crafted than Espíritu Santo. Raiford says the church was made of plastered stone and topped with a shingled roof, and all the buildings in the complex were surrounded by a sturdy stone wall.

After Texas gained its independence from Mexico in 1836, Espíritu Santo and La Bahía became the property of the Republic of Texas. When Goliad was incorporated in 1840, the city claimed the mission and presidio as its own but did little to maintain the structures. They had already begun to fall into disrepair after secularization in 1830, and attempts by the Roman Catholic church to regain ownership were only partially successful. Although the Congress of the Texas Republic passed legislation in 1841 that recognized the church's ownership of the missions in San Antonio and Goliad, the church failed to gain possession of either of the Goliad properties until 1855, when the Goliad city council saw fit to turn the presidio chapel over to the church for "religious purposes." Meanwhile, an ordinance passed by the city council in 1847 allowed citizens to have all the loose stone they could carry from within and around the walls of the presidio and mission. Soon houses and stores built of historic stone began to sprout all around the mission sites. The grounds of Espíritu Santo were eventually turned over to the Presbyterian church for use as Aranama College, which opened in 1858 and

[7]Hal Box, "Texas Traditions: A Sense of Texas Architecture," *Architectural Review* (November, 1978): 267.

The remains of the Espíritu Santo granary, former site of Aranama College. (This photograph was taken during the 1920s.)

The chapel at Mission Espíritu Santo, Goliad. (Photograph by Charles Sappington)

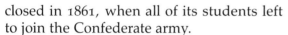
The front door of the chapel at Mission Espíritu Santo, Goliad. (Photograph by Charles Sappington)

The bell tower at Mission Espíritu Santo, Goliad. (Photograph by J. Griffis Smith)

closed in 1861, when all of its students left to join the Confederate army.

By the time Raiford and Vosper began the restoration of Espíritu Santo, the only building of the original mission still standing was the granary, which had recently been restored by the WPA. But Raiford says it was made to look more like a mission building in California than in Texas, and to find out any more about what Espíritu Santo was really like, architecture was going to have to take a back seat to archaeology—for the time being anyway. "That's where I developed a real appreciation for archaeology," Raiford says. It didn't take him long to realize that a thorough scientific investigation of a historic site is absolutely essential in understanding what was built thereon. It is also important to conduct historical research, which can reveal drawings, dates, and facts about buildings to be restored that could only be guessed at otherwise.

To ensure such thoroughness in the restoration of Espíritu Santo, the Park Service assembled an authoritative team: Vosper as chief architect and superintendent; Raiford as project architect; landscape architect Richard Colley, who had been a friend of Raiford's at A&M (and who would go on to make quite a name for himself as a Texas architect as well); project architect Temple Phinney, who had been a student of Vosper's at UT; archaeologist Eric Reed, from the Park Service's Santa Fe office; assistant archaeologist Roland Beard; project engineer Lewis Pettus; and construction foremen Cyrus White and Cecil Craddock. Raiford would also be assisted by researchers Bill Hogan, who had helped him with the Fort Parker reconstruction, and Charles Ramsdell.

Before long, it became clear to the Park Service who was really in charge of the Espíritu Santo restoration. Six months into the

Interior of the chapel at Mission Espíritu Santo, Goliad. (Photograph by Charles Sappington)

project, as Raiford assumed more and more responsibility and Vosper less and less, Raiford was made the superintendent and Vosper one of the project architects. Negotiating bureaucratic rules and regulations, filling out monthly reports, and keeping expenditures within the budget did not suit Vosper, who had great skills as a design architect but few as an administrator. Since the fall of 1931, as Raiford says, when the A&M college architect hired him to come back and look after Vosper, Raiford had become Vosper's "general manager." In any event, Vosper couldn't have been happier about his demotion, and Raiford, all of

twenty-five years of age, was now in charge of the whole Espíritu Santo project, including the maintenance and care of thousands of dollars worth of Park Service equipment and two CCC companies made up entirely of World War I veterans.

Relying on clues and artifacts from the site excavations, along with information on the Spanish missions provided by researcher Ramsdell, who spent most of his time down in Mexico, Raiford and his crew were able to restore three of the stone buildings that formed the mission compound. According to Raiford, one rule of thumb in figuring how high the walls were was to determine

The end of the arcade at Mission Espíritu Santo, Goliad. (Photograph by Charles Sappington)

Exposed stone in a plastered wall at Mission Espíritu Santo, Goliad. (Photograph by J. Griffis Smith)

Hound's-tooth serration atop a wall at Mission Espíritu Santo, Goliad. (Photograph by J. Griffis Smith)

Detail, Mission Espíritu Santo, Goliad. (Photograph by J. Griffis Smith)

how far the stone lay from the wall line. The distance from the farthest stone to the wall line, generally speaking, represented the same distance from the ground to the top of the wall when the wall was intact. Another principle that held true at Espíritu Santo, he says (as it generally did in other mission restorations), was that the ceiling height was one and one-half times the distance between the walls. Among the artifacts discovered at Espíritu Santo were traces of mercuric oxide, a compound ranging in color from ochre to deep red that the Indians used to paint their pottery and faces. It is found in Texas only in the Big Bend area, indicating what a valuable commodity it must have been to Indians of the coastal plain. (To this day, Raiford uses mercuric oxide as a base for some of his watercolors.)

In August of 1937, while Raiford was restoring Espíritu Santo, the Texas legislature passed the state's first architect registration law, prompted in part by the tragic New London disaster the previous March in which 293 schoolchildren were killed when their schoolhouse was leveled by a gas explosion. Always something of a learned profession, architecture had yet to become as regulated, prestigious, or lucrative as medicine or law, at least not in Texas. Regardless of education, anyone could hang out a shingle and design buildings; experience was traditionally had by apprenticeship, although a term or two at the Ecole des Beaux-Arts or any other architecture school would always help.

Actually, efforts to "professionalize" the practice of architecture had been under way in Texas since 1889, when the Texas State Association of Architects proposed a bill to appoint a licensing board for architects. Had the bill been voted upon and passed (it was introduced in the House but never called for a vote), it would have been one of the first state architect registration laws in the country. As it was, the postponed bill was considered a model law by other states,

Raiford (*center*) with Eleanor Roosevelt at Mission Espíritu Santo in 1936.

which proceeded to pass their own licensing laws. By 1937, Texas turned out to be one of the last states to enact such a law, which included a grandfather clause allowing those who were practicing architecture at the time of its passage to receive a license without taking the exam. (Today, the Texas law is considered rather toothless, since the license only grants the use of the title "architect"; anyone can lawfully design any kind of building in Texas as long as he doesn't call himself an architect.)

With a degree in architecture, and having worked as a building draftsman and designer since 1931, Raiford applied for and received Texas license number 198. As he likes to say of his becoming a registered Texas architect, with claim to all the titles and privileges thereunto pertaining, "I now had a license to starve to death on my own terms."

All the while Raiford was working on Espíritu Santo, he had his eyes on another potential project—the restoration of Presidio La Bahía. The mission may have symbolized the more noble aspects of Spanish colonialism in Texas, but it didn't have the place in Texas lore that the presidio did. Not quite the shrine that the Alamo had become (the restoration of which was begun in 1912), La Bahía was nevertheless "the Texan home for Melpomene," as historian Joe B. Frantz writes. "No buskined Athenian could have created a more congenially menacing stage for the muse of tragedy than those Franciscan fathers from Zacatecas who chose La Bahía to introduce the sunshine of this world and the next to the undesiring aborigine."[8]

In fact, most everyone involved in the Goliad preservation projects was more interested in restoring La Bahía than either of the missions. According to Raiford, the Reverend Mariano S. Garriga, bishop of the diocese in Corpus Christi that had jurisdiction over the presidio, was all for it, as was Judge J. A. White, chairman of the Goliad State Park Commission. The idea was to restore the mission, which originally was the main church complex, and trade it to the Catholic church for the presidio, which originally was the main military complex. La Bahía would then be made into a historic Texas shrine like the Alamo. But Bishop Garriga could not convince the church that restoring the presidio would serve its religious purpose, since the presidio chapel, Nuestra Señora de Loreto, with its prized statue of Our Lady of Loreto, was still very much in use as a parish church.

The Historic Sites Act of 1935 was designed in part to ameliorate such conflict for the sake of a higher purpose. One section of the act empowered the Department of the Interior to enter into cooperative agreements with private organizations for the preservation of designated National Historic Sites. But that part of the law was effective mainly when the federal government owned the site and allowed private groups to use it; rarely did it work in reverse. And once again, nowhere would this issue arise more intensely than with Maury Maverick in San Antonio—this time over the restoration of Mission San José y San Miguel de Aguayo. The issue was complicated in this case by multiple ownership: The Catholic church held title to and used the mission church and the San Antonio Conservation Society and Bexar County owned the mission grounds. There was also some reluctance on the part of the National Park Service to involve itself in the San José project since restoration had already begun as a local effort under the guidance of San Antonio architect Harvey P. Smith, with the help of WPA labor and funds. Although it recognized San Jose's historical and architectural value (called "Queen of the Texas Missions," it is considered as fine an example of the Mexican Baroque as you can find anywhere in Mexico), the Park Service could not endorse work that it hadn't researched and authenticated. Then in the spring of 1936, the Texas Centennial Commission agreed to appropriate a paltry twenty thousand dollars to finish the restoration of San José, which made the Park Service even more reluctant to get involved. Well aware of the concurrent Goliad projects, according to historian Charles Hosmer, Maverick was displeased that Espíritu Santo was "developed so well" and San José was "left to just lie there and rot to pieces."[9] Maverick was certain that San José was potentially a far better draw for tourists, and he could not understand why the Park Service could demonstrate such expertise at Espíritu Santo and not at San José or how

[8]Joe B. Frantz et al., *Six Missions of Texas* (Waco: Texian Press, 1965), p. 57.

[9]Hosmer, *Preservation Comes of Age* I, 692.

church ownership could hamper federal involvement in such a noble cause.

In spite of the church's reluctance to barter with the Goliad preservationists over La Bahía, Raiford could not keep his mind off the presidio. Since the mission and the presidio were of the same architectural vintage, he had to study both to learn about either one. Then in the fall of 1937, piquing his interest in La Bahía even more, an "unassuming tourist" from Lakemont, New York, named James P. Long walked into Raiford's office at the Espíritu Santo site. According to Raiford, the man "displayed an unusual interest in the restoration work being done," mentioning in conversation that his wife was related to Capt. Joseph M. Chadwick, Fannin's adjutant who was in charge of fortifying the presidio. Long claimed that his wife, whose maiden name was Chadwick, had a drawing of the presidio that had been handed down in the Chadwick family. Raiford expressed a definite interest in seeing it, and upon Long's return to New York, he mailed Raiford a photostatic copy. His cover letter, dated December 3, 1937, concluded with: "We hope that you will find this of value in your research and that you may get a chance to restore the fort."[10]

In subsequent correspondence with Long's wife, Raiford learned that the drawing, a bird's-eye perspective made by a New York lithographer in 1836 and entitled "The Correct View of Fort Defiance," was based on a smaller, 6-by-6-inch drawing that Chadwick had sent his mother in his last letter from Goliad. The larger lithograph showed a pitched-roofed, Gothic chapel, which meant that the New York lithographer had never seen a Spanish colonial structure. But the notes on the lithograph were remarkably thorough, describing the uses of various rooms and buildings and indicating how detailed Chadwick's original draw-

Watercolor portrait of Capt. Joseph M. Chadwick, painted by famous frontier artist George Catlin.

ing—which Raiford thought was probably an annotated plan—must have been. As Raiford points out, Chadwick had undergone two years of military and engineering training at West Point, had worked as a draftsman in the Missouri Land Office before coming to Texas in 1835, and had supervised the improvements made to the presidio under Fannin's command. So it was not surprising that Chadwick's original drawing, from all indications, must have been "remarkably accurate as to orientation, line, dimensions, and relations of the various components of the plan."[11]

For the time being, the only significance the lithograph had was in settling arguments among presidio devotees as to where the main entrance was in 1836 and how

[10] Kathryn Stoner O'Connor, *The Presidio La Bahía del Espíritu Santo de Zuñiga, 1721 to 1846* (Austin: Von Boeckmann-Jones, 1966), p. 199.

[11] Ibid., p. 200.

Watercolor of the reconstructed capitol at Williamsburg done by Raiford after visiting the site with his mother and sisters in 1937.

prevalent *jacal* structures were in and around the compound. According to the lithograph, the main entrance was on the south side, and the presidio and its environs were made up entirely of stone structures. Although it seemed unlikely that the church would allow the presidio to be made into a state historic site anytime soon, Raiford would have loved to have laid his hands on Chadwick's original 6-by-6-inch drawing, and he would grow ever more curious about its existence. Was it moldering in a Chadwick attic somewhere? Could it ever be found? Drawing or no drawing, would Raiford ever get a chance to restore La Bahía?

Meanwhile, as he continued to work on other Goliad projects, Raiford continued to keep in generous touch with his family. The depression had been hard on East Texas and on Raiford's father, but thanks to the New Deal, Raiford was doing relatively well down in Goliad, and he couldn't resist spending money on or time with his loved ones. His oldest sister Frances shares an excerpt from a letter Raiford wrote her on September 12, 1937, upon her matriculation at UT: "Dear Sister: Well I guess you are about ready to wend your way to the Capitol city and school. I am glad you are going to the University as I know it is a good school and you will be near us all as well as its being a place where you can have a good time and make contacts that will be of real value to you later. . . . I am enclosing a check for $25 and some blanks for you to use as you need them. I am sorry that I am not fixed to give you more but want you to know that I am all for you and will help in any way I can. Your brother, Raiford."[12]

Frances also remembers that, late one spring during the Espíritu Santo restoration, Raiford bought his mother a new car. He then drove his mother and three younger sisters to Washington, D.C., where Frances was in school, to bring Frances to Texas for the summer. On the way back they stopped in Williamsburg and Raiford did a watercolor of the reconstructed capitol (which hangs now in his San Augustine office). Back in Texas, he invited Frances down to Goliad, where she spent the summer typing specifications for the mission restoration and the construction of a caretaker's house for the state historical park, of which the mission would be a part. When her summer job was finished, they piled into a pickup and headed to Refugio to celebrate, taking a shortcut across "O'Connor's Prairie" (part of the vast O'Connor Ranch). The shortcut would have cut ten miles off the journey had the pickup not become stuck in the mud ten miles out of Goliad. Everyone had to get out of the truck and trudge through the mud and the pitch-dark night to find help. To make matters worse, Frances remembers, "there were herds of cattle all over and we would hear them coming towards us. Raiford had a gun and fired it in the air to divert them. We finally found a tenant's home, but his old Chevrolet wouldn't run. Raiford figured out that the problem was in the gas line, disconnected it, sucked the gasoline out of it and replaced it, then we went back to Goliad."

During his six-year stay in Goliad before the war, working with Vosper on one Park Service job after another, Raiford felt at home. He had been given some good advice when he first came to town in 1935. In-structing Raiford on how best to behave, as he told Katy Capt, the county judge said: "Well, son, you come from an old town— old San Augustine—and you oughta understand the people from Goliad. And I'll tell you how to get along down here. We operate on the principle that your friends can do no wrong. And the other people can't do a goddam thing."[13] Raiford made a lot of friends in Goliad, in part because of the judge's advice and in part because of his own charm. As in college, he was known as "Strip," and he came to be a town fixture. Everyone liked him, even though they didn't seem particularly interested in what he was doing there. Raiford remembers that the townspeople largely ignored all the restoration projects going on around them, having grown up with the history of the town and taking it pretty much for granted. While he was restoring the mission, Raiford says, "all the local people knew what was going on and they more or less appreciated it, but they really couldn't particularly give a damn. They wouldn't come out and see what in the hell we were doing."

One resident of Goliad, however, paid quite a bit of attention to the dashing young architect from San Augustine who was in charge of it all. In the summer of 1940, Raiford met a young woman from Junction named Roberta Ragland. Her parents had both died, and she had come to Goliad after graduating from high school to live with a great-aunt and -uncle. When Roberta and Raiford met, she was twenty and working as a receptionist and nurse in a doctor's office in Goliad, and he was thirty and still a very good dancer as well as a dashing young architect. Their courtship lasted about a year and a half, and in February of 1942 they were married in San Antonio, in the home of one of Roberta's cousins.

Shortly before his marriage, Raiford had begun to explore Mission Rosario. Site excavations revealed that the complex, in its

---

[12]Frances Hartley, letter to author, March 20, 1984.

[13]Capt. "Raiford Leak Stripling," p. 30.

final form as a working mission, had been built of stone laid with clay instead of lime mortar, with which most of the stone missions were constructed. Raiford also discovered that the stone walls had been not only plastered but also decorated with colorful patterns, which debunked the popular notion of the Spanish missions as having always been a dull, earthy gray.

Raiford was excavating Rosario when the Japanese bombed Pearl Harbor, in December of 1941, and Roosevelt redirected national priorities from recovering from a depression to winning a war. Although some of the New Deal programs continued into the war years, military mobilization soon depleted the ranks of the CCC and the NYA, and appropriations for public works projects dwindled accordingly. A lot had been accomplished in the field of historic preservation since the Williamsburg restoration in the late twenties—and particularly since the passage of the Historic Sites Act in 1935—but the long-built-up momentum of

the movement was finally petering out. Working with the Park Service and the state of Texas, Raiford had accomplished quite a bit himself since 1935, and he too felt the preservation movement subside—but he wasn't going to give up without a fight. He had $150,000 worth of trucks and tools and a labor force that was ready to drop everything and go home, but before they did he ordered them to carefully cover up the ruins of Mission Rosario, which they had just finished *uncovering*. Raiford was certain that, left exposed, the mud mortar would deteriorate in no time. It was a good decision, but also an unauthorized one, and Raiford soon caught personal, "unmitigated hell" from Secretary of the Interior Harold Ickes, who was known to have somewhat of a cantankerous personality and administrative style. As Raiford told Katy Capt, "Old man Ickes did everything but put me in jail, and I think he thought about that."[14]

[14] Ibid., p. 33.

CHAPTER 5

Bird Dogs and La Bahía

Raiford had just turned thirty-one when the United States declared war on Japan and Germany, and since there had been no love lost between Raiford and the U.S. Army when he left the A&M Corps of Cadets in 1929, he was in no hurry to contribute to the war effort as an overage infantryman. Like the vast majority of his fellow Americans, however, he wanted to make some kind of patriotic contribution, and being an experienced architect made him a fairly valuable commodity. The war effort involved not only the design and production of military weapons and equipment but also the design and construction of military bases, defense plants, housing, and other war-related facilities—all of which had to be built in short order—which created a strong demand for architects inside the service and out.

The military also found other ways to put architects to work. One of the most exotic was the U.S. Navy camouflage program in Washington, which was actually a three-pronged effort within the Navy Department's Bureau of Ships (BuShips), Bureau of Aeronautics (BuAer), and Bureau of Yards and Docks (BuDocks). The first two concerned themselves with the camouflaging of ships and planes for seagoing and aerial combat, the third with hiding ships at dock-

side and planes parked on land. And all three brought together a colorful assortment of architects, artists, interior designers, set designers, and experts from England, where naval camouflage was first experimented with during World War I.

The idea then, proposed by a young lieutenant in the Royal Naval Reserve who was a peacetime painter and poster designer, was to "break up" the form of a ship with masses of starkly contrasting colors—a technique that came to be called "dazzle-painting"—which was supposed to confuse a U-boat as to the ship's exact course. Between wars the art of seagoing camouflage was not a top priority. Then, in 1935, the U.S. Navy began to experiment with colors and patterns that were put to the test in Lend-Lease convoy escorts before the United States actually entered the war. Eventually it became clear that the camouflage pattern that hid the ship or plane while at sea or in the air made it stand out like a sore thumb when it was tied to a pier or sitting on an airstrip. Enter BuDocks, the bureau within the Navy Department responsible for laying out and building shore facilities. The object of its camouflaging efforts would relate closely to that of Pratt Institute's in New York—where Vosper had studied architecture—which set up an in-

Samuel Charles Phelps Vosper, photographed by Raiford, celebrating his birthday in Washington, D.C., 1944.

dustrial camouflage laboratory in its department of architecture in September of 1940, headed by architect Konrad Wittman.

When the Japanese bombed Pearl Harbor, Vosper had already moved to Washington, where he was designing post offices for the Treasury Department, and in early 1942 he called Raiford to tell him of an opening in this new BuDocks division. Raiford took the job, closing down the Goliad office for the duration and moving with Roberta to Washington immediately after their marriage, taking along an Irish setter bird dog named

"Miss Tucker" and staying with Raiford's younger brother Robert and his wife Essie for several weeks until they found an apartment in Alexandria, Virginia. (By then, Robert was working in Washington as the chief investigator for the Un-American Activities Committee.)

There were some forty people on staff in the BuDocks camouflage section at the Washington Navy Yard, Raiford recalls, most of whom were civilian employees of the Navy, including the first women architects he had ever encountered. Raiford was eventually assigned to work as an assistant to Lt. Cmdr. Charles E. Peterson, whom Raiford had known when Peterson worked for the Park Service out of its regional office in Santa Fe. (Peterson, a Philadelphia architect, would later become a prominent preservationist affiliated with Columbia University in New York.) Raiford and Peterson made a good team. They had worked together on several Park Service projects before the war and had become friends. So as Raiford helped Peterson test various camouflage techniques, he could also help him work around his deathly fear of flying. During one project, as he told Katy Capt, "We'd take these airplane hides [camouflage netting for land-based aircraft]—they'd be made by naval prisoners—and experiment with 'em and photograph 'em and everything down at Quantico at the Marine base. But Peterson hated to fly—he didn't want to have anything to do with an airplane. So we wound up with another tactic. We would take 'em down to the Washington Monument and set 'em up and Mr. Peterson and I would go on up to the top of the monument and photograph 'em from the top of the monument. There wasn't any flyin' involved."[1] Along with other architects in the section, Raiford was eventually put to work planning advanced naval bases and analyzing the plans of factories built in Japan by American companies before the war to determine their most vulnerable points for bombing attacks.

Before the end of the war, on March 22, 1943, a son was born to Raiford and Roberta, Raiford Ragland Stripling, who would be nicknamed "Raggy." He was supposed to be delivered in a hospital in Virginia, which would have made him a Southerner, but plans were changed at the last minute, and Raggy was forced to come into this world a

Roberta, Raggy, and the bird dog "Miss Tucker" in Maryland, 1945.

Yankee at Garfield Memorial Hospital in Washington.

Although born a Yankee, Raggy would escape being reared as one. At war's end, the Raiford Striplings returned with Vosper to Texas, arriving in Goliad on Christmas Day, 1945. It was good to be back in Goliad, but it proved difficult for Raiford to pick up where he and Vosper left off before the war. The Texas centennial had come and gone, and Park Service preservation was no longer the sure-fire source of work that it had been during the depression. Without a government-funded mission restoration under way, Goliad became just another small South Texas town, not exactly the kind of place where architects were in great demand. Raiford soon lost touch with Vosper, who moved to Bryan to work in the office of architect Phil Norton, whom he knew from his A&M days. Like many of Vosper's moves, the one to Bryan was without his wife and daughter, who had returned to Staten Island dur-

---

[1] Katy Capt, "Raiford Leak Stripling: The Life and Times of an East Texas Restoration Architect" (master's thesis, Texas A&M University, 1981), p. 34.

ing the war, never to join Vosper again on
any of his Texas wanderings. (According to
Vosper's son Bradley, his mother always said
her husband, whom she never divorced,
"was a free soul." In 1947, Vosper moved to
the Panhandle town of Pampa to work with
another friend from his A&M days, architect Royal Cantrell, but by 1951, when
Bradley graduated from UT, he had moved
on to San Antonio to work again for Ralph
Cameron. Bradley himself took a job in
Cantrell's office in Pampa, where he had
worked one college summer, and in 1955 he
went to San Antonio to get his dad, who
had suffered several strokes and was living
at the Elks Lodge. Samuel Charles Phelps
Vosper died in Pampa on February 10, 1958,
at the age of sixty-nine.)

As the restoration business dried up in
postwar Goliad, Raiford—as his beloved
mentor was wont to do—took to drink. It
was an inclination that he had playfully in-
dulged and controlled since college, but
Vosper's departure, the drain on his finances, and the inescapable fact that an excit-
ing era had indeed drawn to a close, all took
their toll on Raiford. Finally, in the fall of
1947 Raiford and Roberta were divorced,
due to "insurmountable differences," according to Roberta, who remarried and now
lives in Fulton. She is quick to add, however, that there was absolutely no animosity
between them and that they have remained
friends ever since. According to Raggy, his
mother always had a great affinity and admiration for his father. "She said he was a
genius but that he was never meant to be
married; he was just too much of a free
spirit."

Raggy and his mother moved to Victoria,
where she would marry Howard Garner,
who worked for Truckline Gas Company
and who would love and rear Raggy as his
own. Worried about his older son, Raif
Stripling talked Raiford into returning to
San Augustine to practice architecture. Although San Augustine in the late 1940s

probably wasn't any more conducive to a
prosperous architectural practice than Goliad was, it was home for Raiford, and it
offered him a secure foundation for restoring his life. Meanwhile, during the years
Raggy lived with Roberta and Howard in
Victoria, Raiford visited their home frequently, and Raggy would spend the summers and Christmases with his father in San
Augustine, where Raiford lived alone in a
tiny two-bedroom apartment behind his
parents' house. "When I was a kid," Raggy
says, "Daddy would come down to Victoria
and visit, and I can remember the absolute
hurt that I felt when he left. I wanted to be
with him. He never spanked me, never laid
a hand on me. Of course, I loved my mother,
and it wasn't that I didn't want to be with
her, but he was just my idol, my hero and
everything."

In 1957, when Raggy was fourteen, Howard was transferred to a small town in Louisiana, and he reluctantly moved with them.
Raggy loved his childhood years in Victoria.
It was a growing town with a good school
system and just big and dynamic enough to
turn Raggy into something of a city boy.
Raggy also loved his father, and in the back
of his mind a plan was forming to live with
him in San Augustine, which may not have
been a city like Victoria, but as far as Raggy
was concerned, it offered much more than
any small town in Louisiana ever could. In
addition to having his father, San Augustine had grandparents, Stripling's Drugstore, and the same fields and forests that
his father had romped in as a boy and still
knew like the back of his hand. Biding his
time, Raggy lived in Louisiana for a year
and a half, then one day when he was a
sophomore in high school he announced to
his mother that he was going to go live with
his father. Roberta knew it was inevitable,
Raggy says, and she offered no argument.
So in January of 1959, between semesters
during his sophomore year, Raggy packed
his bags and moved to San Augustine to live

with Raiford, who was living and practicing in the old Stephen W. Blount House, one of the three houses built by Augustus Phelps still standing in San Augustine and one of the finest examples of Greek Revival architecture in Texas (see chapter 6). Raiford purchased the house in 1953 for use as home and office, and by 1959—stuffed full of antique furniture—it was serving as a kind of bachelor pad for Raiford and Raggy and would eventually gain a certain notoriety as the local "YMCA."

Raiford always had a way with kids. From the time Raggy arrived in 1959 to the time he graduated from San Augustine High School in 1961, the Blount House invariably had a teenage boy or two spending the night or just hanging around with Raggy and his dad. Raiford often cooked meals for the boys, talked with them in ways that their own fathers could not, and generally provided an objective and sympathetic adult presence of the sort that teenage boys can value very highly. Young people have always liked him, Raggy says, in part because of his "infinite patience." Some of the mothers around town considered the YMCA to be somewhat less wholesome than the sobriquet would imply, but Raiford would counsel the boys who had problems and make sure that if they insisted on drinking beer, they stayed off the roads and did it at the YMCA, where he could keep an eye on them.

Raiford kicked up his own heels from time to time, often with his good friend Claxton Benedum, nephew of a wealthy wildcatter from Pittsburgh and founder of the Fairway Farm and Hunt Resort a few miles east of town on Highway 21. The two had met through Claxton's wife, the former Sarah Tucker, who had grown up in San Augustine and whom Raiford had known since they were kids. Claxton commissioned Raiford to design their home and clubhouse at Fairway Farms, and before long both were indulging their love of music

together—Claxton on guitar, Raiford on a bass fiddle he had bought in Dallas and taught himself to play. One of their regular gigs was a week in New Orleans, where they would go to the horse races and take in the jazz on Bourbon Street, and once they brought back the entire seven-man band from the Monteleone Hotel to spend a week at the Farms, where the musicians played golf during the day and jammed with Claxton and Raiford long into the night.

Not long after moving into the Blount House, Raiford started seeing an old flame —Marjorie Cavitt, whom he had dated at A&M and with whom he had kept in touch over the years. She was divorced and living in Houston, and one day after Raggy had gone off to A&M and was back home visiting his dad, a friend of Raiford's filled Raggy in on the state of their romance. It seems that one day, the three of them were carousing around San Augustine and having the best time together—until they came back to the Blount House, that is, whereupon Marjorie started rearranging the furniture and generally tidying things up. Raiford and Marjorie had been talking some about marriage, evidently, and without saying a word, Raiford was gone. "He just made his exit," Raggy says, "and that was the end of it. He could see that he couldn't change. And he had told me several times before that a person should only be married once. Maybe that was part of it. Anyway, he lit out when she started moving that furniture—he was just too set in his ways."

Marjorie would later marry a man named Holland McCombs, a veteran journalist who was then the Southwest editor of *Fortune* and *Life* magazines and also an avid bird hunter and bird-dog fancier. Raiford and McCombs became friends, and when the Striplings gathered in Bryan for a Christmas with sister Martha's family in the early 1960s, Raiford, Eddie Phillips, Robert, and Robert's wife Essie drove in separate cars out to the Cavitt family plantation house ten miles outside of Bryan on the Camino Real near Wheelock. They spent most of the afternoon out by the bird-dog pens, Robert recalls, telling war stories about their hunting exploits and lying about their dogs. Then McCombs asked Raiford, "Strip, what was the best bird dog you ever owned?" Raiford went on and on about his beloved "Old Joe." Then Raiford asked McCombs the same question, and McCombs waxed romantically about "Old Blue," pointing out the very pen in which he had kept the legendary bird dog until his death a year before. "I hunted him for ten years," McCombs said, "and you know what, Strip? In all those years, Old Blue never let a bird hit the ground. Every bird I killed he caught in his mouth." Robert says Raiford knew he had been had, and he never said a word. He just lit a cigarette, got in his car, and drove 165 miles back to San Augustine.

Raiford's architectural practice, not exactly a booming business, was just right for a man who was inclined to drop everything he was doing when bird season came in the fall and spend weeks at a time with his bird dogs and hunting buddies. It was a welcome change of pace for Raiford. Although he had owned a bird dog continuously since he was eight years old, he hadn't had the flexibility to hunt to his heart's content since he went away to college. Now, on his own in San Augustine and with his Park Service and Navy Department work behind him, Raiford could structure his life around bird season. From the first of the year until late summer, he would practice architecture in his office in a corner bedroom of the Blount House, then spend the balance of the year hunting dove and quail all over Texas, leaving Raggy to be looked after by his grandparents and Eddie Phillips.

Raiford's band of brothers, with whom he shared many a hunting exploit, included Melvill Ingram, Nolan Miller, and George Barham. Raiford likes to tell how Miller was chased from one field three times in a single day, and how Barham once cautioned a man who was running him off his land, "Don't call me an S.O.B., you old S.O.B., I've got a gun in my hand."

One of Raiford's closest hunting buddies was still Peter Payne, "the professor of the bird-dog academy." One day in the fall of 1961, when they were hunting quail together in a grassy clear-cut just outside of town, they jumped a covey and killed two or three birds. They watched where they went down, and as they went after them, Raiford stopped to light a cigarette. Just as he struck the match and brought it to his mouth, another bird—one they had missed when the covey first came up—burst from the grass near Raiford, who instinctively dropped the match, swung around, and killed the quail with one shot. Before they could pick up any of the birds, the match had set the grass on fire, and Peter and Raiford both tried to put the fire out. Peter was wearing waterproof hunting pants lined with rubber and tied tightly around the tops of his boots, and as he stomped on the burning grass, his pants caught fire, the rubber melting on the inside and searing the skin on both legs beneath the knee. "I looked and a blaze was coming out from under my skin," Peter recalls. "And I hollered for Raiford and he run down yellin', 'Unbuckle your pants! Unbuckle your pants!' I laid down and unbuckled them and he just grabbed and pulled them off, then carried me to the doctor."

Payne was so badly injured, with third-degree burns on both legs, that the county hospital called for a plane to fly him to the burn unit at Brooke Army Medical Center in San Antonio. During the first operation on his legs, he suffered a heart attack. Then when he came home, two weeks later, a blood clot dislodged, and he was rushed back to San Antonio. All the while, Payne says, Raiford was sick with worry, sometimes sleeping in his hospital room and frequently driving with Raggy back and forth to San Antonio to keep tabs on his recovery.

When he was practicing architecture, most of Raiford's commissions during his first few years back in San Augustine were new designs—houses, schools, churches, small commercial buildings. And although clients weren't exactly beating a path to his door, he was enough of a rarity in Deep East Texas to attract a loyal following. Outside of the larger towns within a forty-five-mile radius of San Augustine—Lufkin, Nacogdoches, Carthage, and Jasper—there were few registered architects, and the Stripling name was known to be a good one. Then in 1952, his preservation work in Goliad led to a commission to restore one of San Augustine's historic homes, the Ezekiel Cullen House (see chapter 6), another Greek Revival masterpiece built in 1839 by Augustus Phelps. The project would renew Raiford's involvement in historic preservation at a time when the movement was at a definite turning point, and although he would continue to design houses, schools, churches, and small commercial buildings, Raiford would never again be known as "just" an architect.

"It would be no exaggeration to refer to the preservation field of 1949 as mature," writes Charles Hosmer.[2] Indeed, that was the year the National Trust for Historic Preservation was chartered in Washington to coordinate the continuing efforts of the National Park Service as well as private historical societies across the country. But the historic preservation movement that had been eclipsed by the war effort would reemerge in a different light. While postwar prosperity had brought a renewed organizational emphasis to the movement on the national level, Modernism also had a firm grip on American towns and cities, and the International Style building boom of the 1950s

and 1960s—together with the architectural clear-cutting of urban renewal—removed much of the country's most historic urban fabric. And local historical societies, even with the help of the National Trust, could prove somewhat ineffective in the face of such "progress"; commercial pressures were intense in razing whole blocks of historic building stock and "modernizing" ornate Victorian storefronts with blank sheets of plaster and aluminum.

Nevertheless, the cadre of professional preservationists who had come of age during the depression continued to spread the gospel, and as Raiford became less involved with the Park Service on federally funded projects, he became more involved with private projects, which the National Trust encouraged. Between 1952 and 1962 in San Augustine, Raiford did more than anyone else to stimulate an awareness and appreciation of his hometown's architectural riches. He was a leader in organizing the San Augustine County Historical Society and served as chairman of the local committee that worked with the Texas State Historical Survey Committee designating some thirty-four historic structures in the county as Recorded Texas Historic Landmarks. He also spearheaded a drive to reconstruct Mission Nuestra Señora de los Dolores, which highway department archaeologists are now investigating (the site lies in the middle of a highway right-of-way on the outskirts of town). Unlike most members of small-town heritage societies, however, Raiford had an ace up his sleeve: not only could he crusade in the name of historic preservation, he could also *do* it. In addition to the Cullen House, he restored the Blount House, the Milton Garrett House, the Horn-Polk House, the Matthew Cartwright House, the Columbus Cartwright House, the T. N. B. Greer House, the Dunn House, the Herring House, Christ Episcopal Church, and the Old Jail, all in San Augustine and all for private owners (see chapter 6).

[2]Charles B. Hosmer, Jr., *Preservation Comes of Age: From Williamsburg to the National Trust, 1926–1949* (Charlottesville: University Press of Virginia, 1981), I, 7.

Just as one of the first preservation projects in the country was undertaken by a group of farsighted women—the restoration of Mount Vernon in 1859 by the Mount Vernon Ladies' Association—so too would many of the local projects after World War II. Traditionally, most nonprofit preservation groups have been made up mainly of prominent women of a community—or the wives of prominent men—who had enough time and inclination to contribute to worthy causes. In fact, one of the first and most important efforts to save a historic building in Texas was undertaken in 1903 by Clara Driscoll of Austin, who bought a thirty-day option on the Alamo and prevented it from being demolished. In 1905, the state legislature turned the Alamo over to the Daughters of the Republic of Texas (DRT), which also assumed custodianship of the architecturally unique Old Land Office Building in Austin in 1917. By 1924, two years before the start of the Colonial Williamsburg restoration, thirteen San Antonio women had formed the San Antonio Conservation Society for the immediate purpose of saving the old Market House, a Greek Revival building that was torn down anyway. Undaunted, the Society—which would turn out to be one of the most "can-do" preservation groups in the country—turned its attention to saving the Big Bend portion of the San Antonio River, inspiring the River Walk beautification project that architect Hugman would conceive in the thirties, and would later be instrumental in preserving La Villita and Mission San José. As historian Charles Hosmer writes, men did not contribute much to the local effort, at least not in San Antonio and not even in the thirties. With the exception of Maury Maverick, Harvey Smith, O'Neil Ford, and "a few harried husbands," the preservation movement in San Antonio "was a woman's world with a pleasant admixture of Latin culture that the Park Service people avoided when pro-

posals resembling La Villita were presented to them."[3]

Accordingly, most of the preservation work Raiford did after his Park Service stint in Goliad was commissioned by or for women—the DRT, the Galveston Historical Foundation, the Historic Waco Foundation, the Junior League, a philanthropic female client. "I am enough of my mother's child to be a product of the Old South," he told one symposium. "To me, women are ladies. And in my fifty-year practice, they are the ones who have been doin' it. Restoration and preservation would be suffering if it were not for the ladies, and I think they should be thanked and appreciated."

In the spring of 1963, Raiford was approached by a lady to restore the one historic structure that he had longed to work on since the thirties—Presidio La Bahía. He would consider it the job of his life, and Kathryn Stoner O'Connor "the perfect client." Mrs. O'Connor was a devout Roman Catholic from Victoria who had also been interested for years in restoring the presidio. She had been born and reared in that part of the country and had been inspired to write a history of the fort by the recollections of an old friend, Nellie Borland-Wood-Kreisle, whose grandmother and great-grandmother were refugees at La Bahía when Fannin and his troops were there. Now up in years and having devoted much of her adult life to researching the history of the presidio, Mrs. O'Connor was finally able to convince the church—with the help of Bishop Garriga—that restoring it would enhance its value and function as a parish church as well as make an invaluable contribution to Texas' heritage. Her persuasive powers were reinforced considerably by her offer to pay for the project. A member of the wealthy O'Connor ranching family, she established the Kathryn O'Connor Founda-

[3]Hosmer, *Preservation Comes of Age* I, 289.

Presidio La Bahía, Goliad. (Photograph by J. Griffis Smith)

tion to ensure that the restoration of Presidio La Bahía would be a first-rate project and that money would, for all practical purposes, be no object. Since Raiford had been so involved in the restoration of the neighboring missions, had done considerable research himself on the presidio, and was developing quite a reputation as one of the best preservation architects in the state, he was the logical choice for the job.

But Raiford wasn't going to just jump at the chance. He and Raggy drove to Victoria in April of 1963 to meet with Mrs. O'Connor in the Victoria Bank and Trust Building. On the way down, Raiford told Raggy, "I'm going to get this job like I want it or I'm not going to take it." Raggy waited in the car as Raiford met with Mrs. O'Connor; her nephew Kemper Williams (who continues to oversee foundation work and has maintained an active interest in historic Goliad); two of her sons; a Catholic bishop; and several priests, lawyers, and accountants. "And on the other side," he says, "wasn't

anybody but me." Raiford wasn't gone very long, as Raggy recalls, and when he came back out to the car he said, "I got it, and I got it just like I wanted." No contract was signed; their agreement was simply outlined in an exchange of letters. Raiford's fee would be 8 percent of the total project cost, plus travel expenses. "She was just tickled to death," Raiford says, almost as much as he was. From start to finish, no stones were left unturned in investigating the site and researching the history of the fort. "Whatever the job required," Raiford says, "Mrs. O'Connor said yes. There were no nos, no take-it-easies—just do it right."

To that end, Raiford practically lived in the presidio for the duration of the project, setting up an office in a trailer parked inside the walls and commuting back and forth to San Augustine from time to time to take care of other business. For four years, from 1963 to 1967, the restoration of Presidio La Bahía was the primary focus of Raiford's energies, and he threw himself into it. Study-

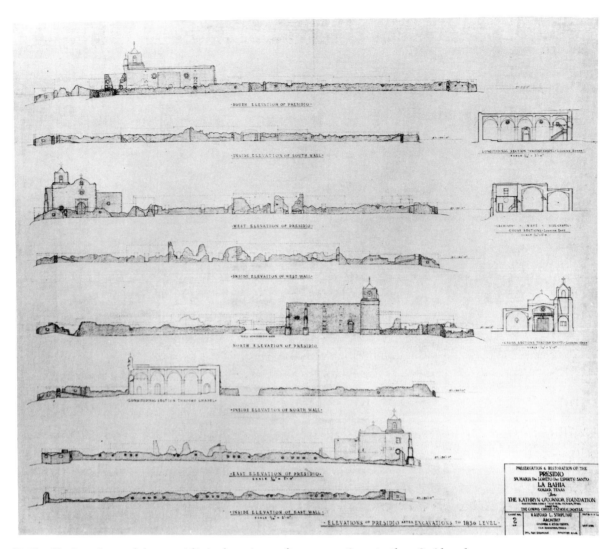

Raiford's drawings of the presidio's elevations after excavations to the 1836 level.

ing architectural engineering at A&M, Raggy would help Raiford in the summers as a draftsman. Other project participants were archaeologist Roland Beard, who had been assistant archaeologist at Espíritu Santo in the thirties; engineer Lewis Pettus, who also had been involved with Espíritu Santo; superintendent O. G. Compton; construction foreman Frank Farley and his wife Rose, who worked for four years as Raiford's secretary; and scores of workmen from the area, many of whom were descendants of

the early inhabitants of La Bahía. Their task, as Mrs. O'Connor writes in her history of the presidio, was to conduct a "preservation and restoration program consisting of the preservation of all existing walls and buildings; thorough archaeological excavation and investigation of the whole site; restoration of the Presidio Compound walls, the Commanding Officers Quarters, Sally-port, Guard House or Calabozo, original Entrances, Bastions, with their ramps, to their condition at the time of Fannin and his Texas

The chapel at Presidio La Bahía in the early 1900s before the belfry was rebuilt by the Knights of Columbus in the 1920s.

army's occupancy in March, 1836, when the most important historic event related to the Presidio La Bahía occurred. . . ."[4]

But there was a limit to how far they would go in restoring the exterior walls. Raiford says that he and Mrs. O'Connor agreed at the outset that the final result should be a "restored ruin," not a completely rebuilt presidio. Although the form and detail of the fort would be re-created, the rebuilt limestone walls would remain

unplastered, even though the evidence of their condition in 1836 indicated otherwise. The idea wasn't to rebuild a brand-new presidio that looked immaculately maintained but to make it look worn as well as whole, so that a visitor's preconceived notions of "visual history" wouldn't be too severely violated.

Restorers began by taking hundreds of photographs to record the conditions of existing walls and structures. Then they divided the site into twenty-foot staked and numbered squares and did a complete archaeological excavation, taking the site down

[4]Kathryn Stoner O'Connor, *The Presidio La Bahía del Espíritu Santo de Zuñiga, 1721 to 1846* (Austin: Von Boeckmann-Jones, 1966), p. 275.

Raiford points out traces of the original polychromatic wainscoting on a plastered interior wall at La Bahía, 1966.

Raiford's watercolor of the polychromatic wainscoting on the plastered interior wall at La Bahía.

Interior of the chapel at Presidio La Bahía, Goliad, showing the groin-vaulted ceiling. (Photograph by J. Griffis Smith)

to its 1836 level. By the time the project began, in April of 1963, most of the compound walls had crumbled into chest-high piles of stone covered with anaqua trees and prickly pear. One arched opening, marking a passageway in what was once the commanding officer's quarters, still stood; all the rest were rubble. The only intact structure was the chapel, which was still functioning as a church and in fairly good repair (although at least one attempt to "restore" it in the late thirties by a well-intentioned Refugio woman resulted in a fresco being painted on the back wall behind the altar, which Raiford says "really disturbs the whole spirit of the chapel" but which was left on the wall nonetheless). Raiford was particularly impressed by the fact that the chapel's unique groin-vaulted ceiling had been supported for years by the four-foot-thick walls alone; buttresses built to carry the thrusts of the vaulted ceiling

had deteriorated over the years because of runoff from the roof. Raiford was also pleased to find that even though the compound walls had crumbled, many sections were still high enough to show beam indentations, which indicated how high the ceilings were in buildings adjacent to the walls.

Working closely with archaeologist Beard and the 1836 lithograph, along with every other description of the fort they could find, Raiford pieced together a detailed image of the presidio not only as it was under Fannin's command but also as it evolved from its original construction as a *jacal* stockade. An estimate made for repairing the presidio, which researchers found in the Bexar Archives of the Barker Texas History Center at the University of Texas, indicated that the compound was enlarged at one point, which was confirmed by the discovery of stone foundations extending from

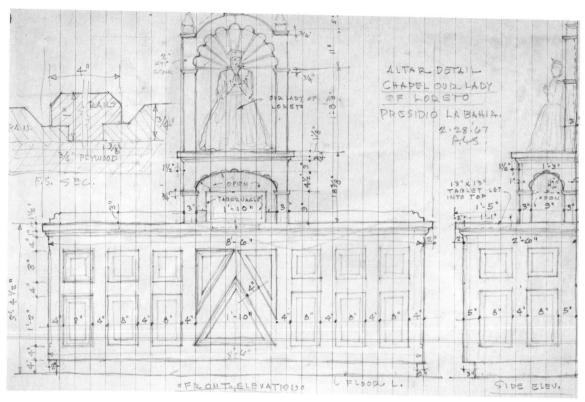

Raiford's sketch of the altar detailing for the chapel at Presidio La Bahía, Goliad.

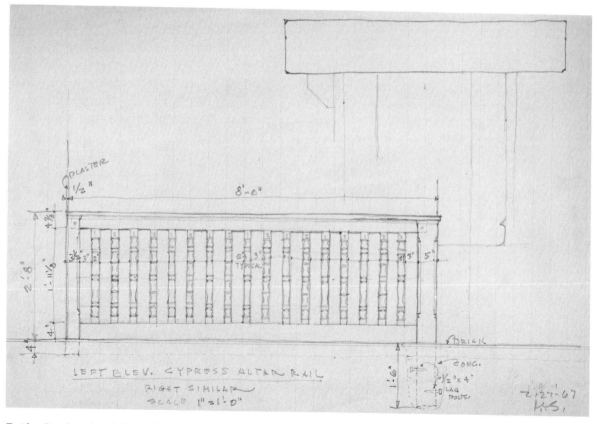

Raiford's sketch of the left-hand portion of the cypress altar rail for the chapel at Presidio La Bahía, Goliad.

Raiford's sketch of the baptismal fount for the chapel at Presidio La Bahía, Goliad.

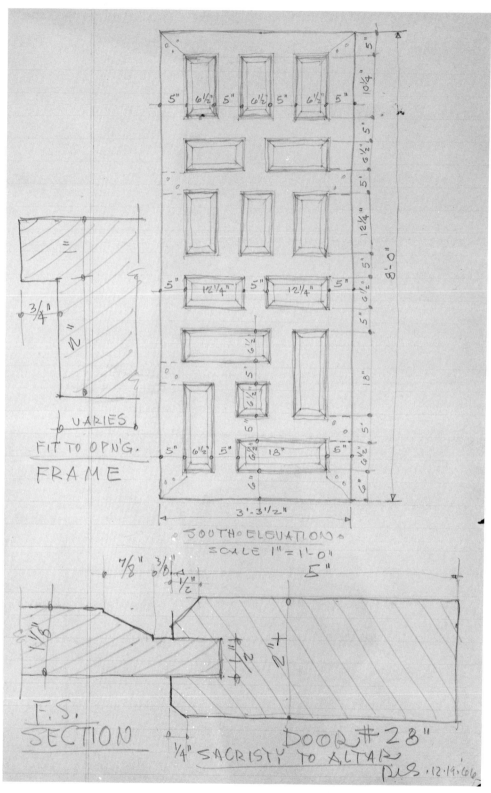

Raiford's sketch of the door leading from the sacristy to the altar for the chapel at Presidio La Bahía, Goliad.

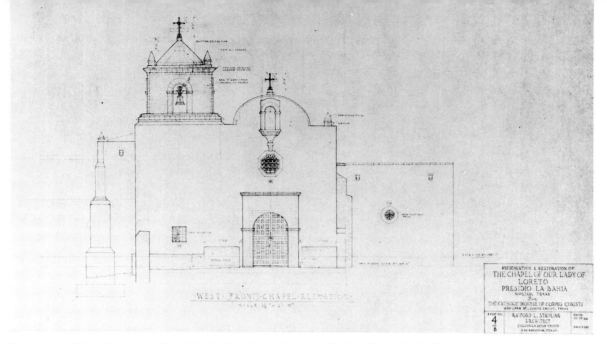

The front of the chapel at Presidio La Bahía, Goliad, with details of the bell tower.

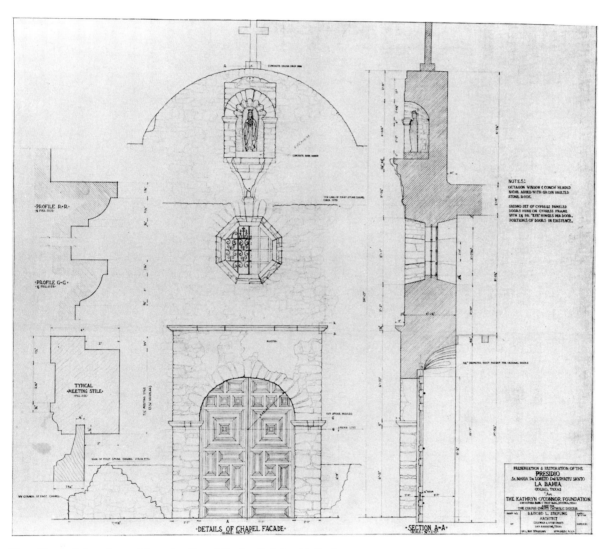

Detailing of the chapel facade, Presidio La Bahía, Goliad.

Front door of the chapel at Presidio La Bahía, Goliad. (Photograph by J. Griffis Smith)

the northeast corner of the commanding officer's quarters to a point some seventy-five feet south of the existing northeast corner of the compound. This meant that the chapel was once situated outside the presidio walls. According to reports from Spanish officers who inspected the presidio in 1750 and 1762, the buildings within the compound during those years (save for the captain's quarters, which was usually built of stone and mortar from the start) were of *jacal* construction, plastered inside and out with caliche mixed with hay or moss. The plaster was intended not so much to finish out the rough-hewn *jacal* as it was to render the buildings fireproof. The chapel itself, from all indications, was originally built in 1749 of plastered *jacal*, with a pole-framed pitched roof covered with thatch or wood shakes. Its second incarnation was that of a stone-walled rectangle with a beamed and shingled roof. The third and final chapel, also built of stone, features what is thought to be the only original groin-vaulted roof structure built by the Spanish still in existence in the Southwest.

Detail of the chapel door at Presidio La Bahía, Goliad. (Photograph by J. Griffis Smith)

Excavations revealed that the main entrance to the compound in Fannin's day was indeed on the south side, as the lithograph indicated. It was also found that the 1836 grade around the various structures was as much as four feet below ground, which had risen over the last 117 years because of the continual accumulation of dirt, vegetation, and structural debris. Areas of the site that had been interior spaces showed as many as four floor lines, ranging from packed earth to kiln-fired tile, and sections of partitions in the commanding officer's quarters had as many as seven layers of plaster and paint. In what was once a room off the command-ing officer's quarters, traces of a colorful wainscoting were found on the original plaster of an excavated wall. According to old photographs as well as openings in the chapel and in the remains of the command-ing officer's quarters, doors and windows were made of a cypress frame topped with a round key-stoned arch (typically Spanish) on the inside and a flat "jack arch" on the outside. There was no indication that wood lintels (also typically Spanish) were ever used. Ash and burned fragments in wall cavities, as well as a hearthstone found in the south wall of the commandant's room, indicated fireplace locations.

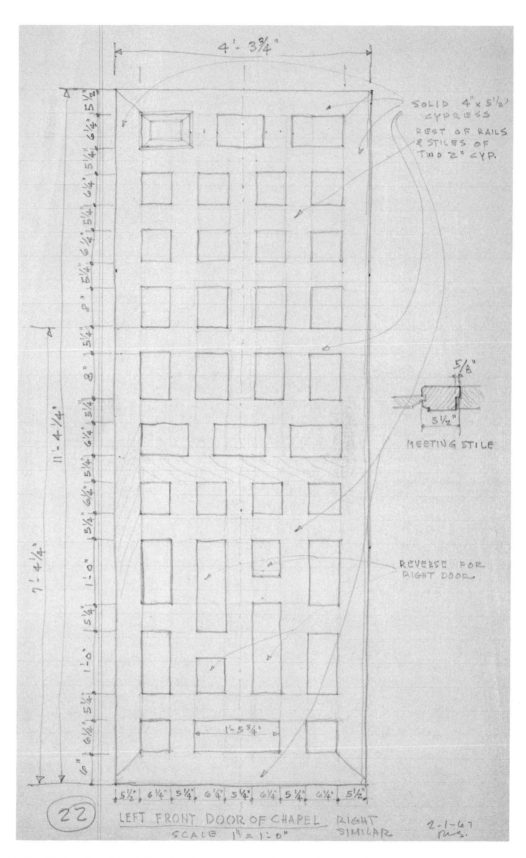

Raiford's sketch of the left side of the cypress door at the Presidio La Bahía chapel, Goliad.

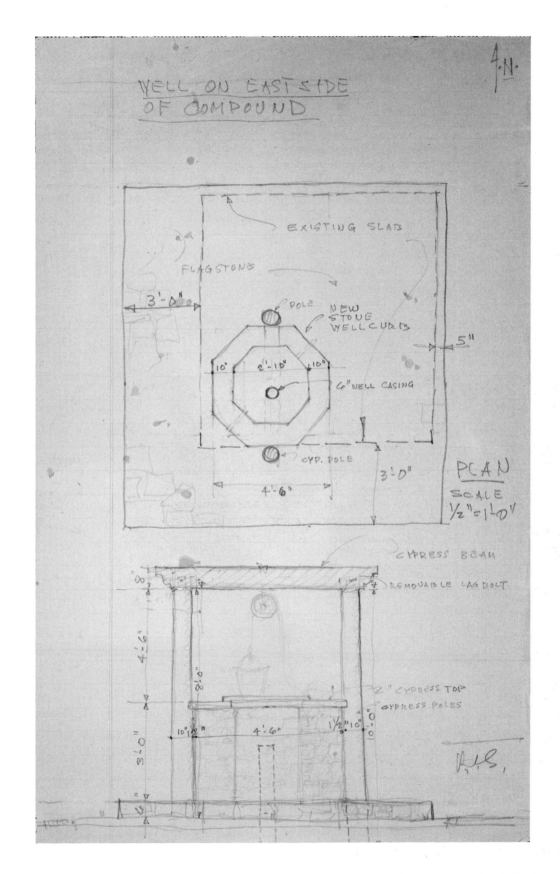

Raiford's sketch for the well on the east side of the Presidio La Bahía compound at Goliad.

Octagonal window with wrought-iron grille above the front door of the chapel at Presidio La Bahía, Goliad. (Photograph by J. Griffis Smith)

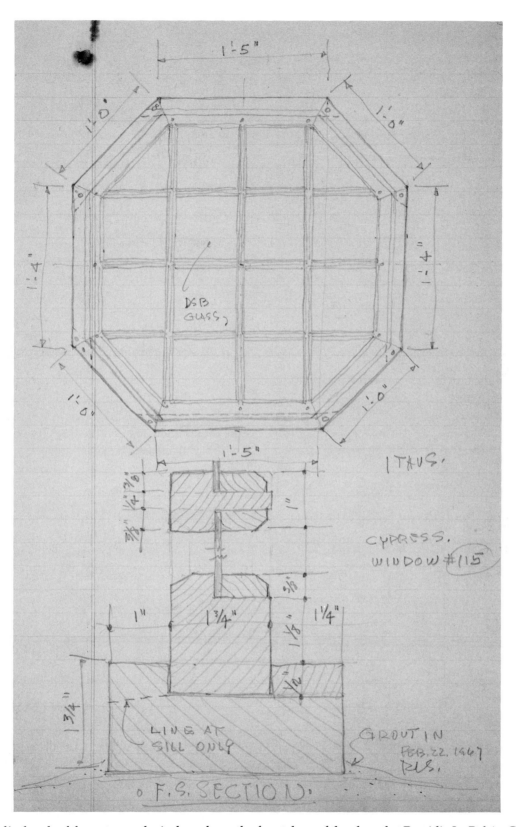

Raiford's sketch of the octagonal window above the front door of the chapel at Presidio La Bahía, Goliad.

Restorers also uncovered a wealth of artifacts, many of which were found in a cistern dug into the caliche sixty feet east of the chapel. (The cistern must have failed as a source of water, archaeologists figured, since it began to be filled with refuse not long after it was dug, sometime around 1775.) This priceless "refuse" found during the restoration, numbering more than four thousand items, included a brass protractor that could very well have belonged to Chadwick, gun parts indicating that Texans and Mexicans alike used variations of the British "Brown Bess," brass candleholders, bell clappers, copper pots, china, square nails, double-eye hinges, and a number of double-sliding flat bolts, which suggested that shutters added to the windows after 1800 had a certain kind of center mullion.

Excavations of the presidio site lasted a year, until April of 1964. From the beginning, however, restoration of the chapel and compound walls continued apace, as did the all-important historical research, which went on well after the site was completely excavated. Mrs. O'Connor wanted an exhaustively thorough job of it, and Raiford was more than happy to oblige. It was a dream project for a preservation architect, something like the Rockefeller-financed restoration of Colonial Williamsburg; Raiford had carte blanche to get at the facts, the pursuit of which was hastened by a nagging unknown. Ultimately, as in the reconstruction of the capitol at Williamsburg—the accuracy of which depended upon the 1929 discovery of a copperplate engraving in the Bodleian Library at Oxford—a factual restoration of La Bahía would depend on whether a certain long-lost image of the presidio could ever be found. As Raiford cautioned Mrs. O'Connor, "We don't dare touch this thing without completely excavating it back to the 1836 level, use all the archaeology that we can buy, do all the research in Mexico and Spain that we can do finding descriptions, documents of any kind—but primarily, don't restore anything until we can prove what was there. Because if we don't do the archaeological work, someday that drawing of Chadwick's is gonna show up and we will all have egg *all over our faces*."

Raiford was still in touch with Chadwick's descendants in New York, who continued to search high and low for the drawing. Meanwhile, to ensure that walls and structures were rebuilt with as much authenticity as he could verify at the time, Raiford conducted a training program for the workmen to acquaint them with techniques used by Spanish colonial stonemasons. Although the main reason the missions and presidios were first built of *jacal* was not so much the scarcity of rock in the mid-eighteenth century as it was the scarcity of rocklayers, such was not the case two hundred years later with the restoration of La Bahía. Descendants of the original mission inhabitants proved proficient at laying limestone with mortar and spalls (slivers of stone wedged into the joints to help stabilize the larger stones), just as the Spanish and Indian stonemasons did when they rebuilt the *jacal* structures, working mainly with their hands and backs. In instructing the workmen, Raiford took a similarly primitive approach. "I would just make a freehand drawing of what I wanted those guys to do," he says, "and just give them a piece of that damn yellow paper and they would work from that. There were no stamps, approved by so-and-so, to bugger 'em—there was nothing technical about it."

Methods and materials used in the restoration were not without some underlying hint of modern technology. To strengthen the walls, workmen installed a reinforced concrete beam as a footing, then filled the gap between interior and exterior walls with quick-set concrete; wood for doors, door and window frames, and window shutters was all treated with a fire retardant and preservative, then sandblasted,

Wrought-iron window grille, Presidio La Bahía, Goliad. (Photograph by J. Griffis Smith)

smoked, and stained to give it a weathered look; floor tiles were laid upon reinforced concrete slabs; roofs consisted of sheet lead, wood decking, and reinforced concrete slabs, all covered with a mixture of white cement, lime, and caliche; and all masonry walls and roofs were coated with a clear waterproofing. Truer to vintage construction techniques, workmen rebuilt both sides of the compound walls and exterior walls of buildings six to ten inches thick with weathered stone and spalls; interior building walls were remade of rubble stone, then plastered and painted; hardware for doors,

gates, and shutters was reproduced to duplicate artifacts discovered on site; and wrought-iron grillwork to protect all the exterior shuttered openings in the compound wall was copied from existing grilles on windows of the chapel as well as those found during the excavation (reproductions by San Antonio metalworker Kurt Voss, whose father did the ornamental metal work for several of Vosper's A&M buildings in the 1930s).

The restoration of La Bahía was completed in September of 1967. Then, two weeks before Secretary of the Interior Stuart

Guard post and chapel at Presidio La Bahía, Goliad. (Photograph by J. Griffis Smith)

Udall and Lady Bird Johnson were to re-dedicate the presidio on October 8, Chadwick's drawing turned up in a library in Charlottesville, Virginia. It was an anxious moment for Raiford, of course, since no matter how exhaustive the research had been, only an image of the fort rendered at the time at which the restoration was aimed could corroborate—or contradict—his four-year, $2 million effort. As it turned out, the restoration appeared to follow Chadwick's drawing to the letter, as if Raiford had been looking at it all along. It is testimony to the importance of archaeological and historical research in historic preservation that so much could be learned of the presidio's evolution just by studying its site and ruins, without the aid of Chadwick's drawing. And Raiford is right to give much of the credit for the project's success to archaeologist Roland Beard, who continued on as a kind of staff archaeologist for the Kathryn O'Connor Foundation. But there is no question that the authenticity of the La Bahía restoration depended largely on Raiford's perseverance, attention to detail, and willingness to get his hands dirty. As Mrs. O'Connor points out in her acknowledg-

ments on the restoration, "Without the enthusiastic interest and work of Mr. Raiford
Stripling and his crew this extremely difficult operation would have been impossible.
Instead of a financial job to be done it has
become to them a labor of love. All their interest and physical labor has been devoted
to it, from the humblest masonry worker
up to the architect-restorer-archaeologist,
Raiford Stripling. The latter has been indefatigable in digging up historical records,
maps, letters, drawings as well as digging
the caliche soil."[5]

After completion of the La Bahía restoration, Raiford returned full-time to his practice in San Augustine and to a backlog of
work, much of which was preservation
projects. By the late 1960s, Raiford had
made quite a name for himself as a preservation architect, and was sought after more
and more as an authority in his field. Between 1967 and 1973, he worked for the
Texas Parks and Wildlife Department as well
as a number of private owners and local
preservation groups in restoring some of
the most historically significant buildings in
Texas, including the Fort House, Earle-
Napier-Kinnard House, East Terrace, and
Earle-Harrison House in Waco; the French
Legation in Austin; Ashton Villa in Galveston; and Independence Hall at Washington-
on-the-Brazos (see chapter 6). In September
of 1969, he also participated in the second
statewide preservation workshop at the University of Texas' Winedale Historical Center
near Round Top entitled "A Conference on
the Principles of Architectural Preservation
and Restoration" and sponsored by UT and
the Texas State Historical Survey Committee. In his presentation at the workshop,
Raiford talked generally about what he
called his "first love," the Greek Revival
style in Texas, and specifically about his
work in Waco, which—along with Austin—
is the last Texas town of those that marked

the western boundary of the Old South to
feature any kind of well-preserved sampling
of Greek Revival homes.

That Raiford began to work mainly for
private clients on the local level did not
mean that the federal government had completely lost interest in historic preservation.
In 1966, President Johnson signed the National Historic Preservation Act, which further encouraged local efforts by setting up a
matching-grant program for the surveying
and restoring of historic sites and the national Advisory Council on Historic Preservation to advise Congress and the president.
Probably the most important outgrowth of
the act was the National Register of Historic
Places, which is administered on the national level by the National Park Service and
on the local level in Texas by the Texas Historical Commission (THC). Texas properties
are selected for the Register on the basis of
their "significance in American history,
architecture, archaeology and culture" by
the State Board of Review, a committee
appointed by the THC executive director
and composed of citizens from across the
state with some expertise in history, architecture, archaeology, and the fine arts.[6]
The THC, established in 1953 as the Texas
State Historical Survey Committee, also pro-
mulgates preservation guidelines on the
state level and conducts a comprehensive
historical-marker program, which recog-
nizes a historic structure or site by affixing
the familiar medallion with interpretive
plate and designating it a Recorded Texas
Historic Landmark.

As the preservation movement became
more of a local effort again—only this time
with the professional support of the National Park Service and National Trust—
there also came certain adjustments in ways
of interpreting and preserving historic architecture. Since the 1930s, when architec-

[5] Ibid., p. vii.

[6] *The National Register of Historic Places in Texas* (Austin: Texas Historical Commission, 1979), p. 7.

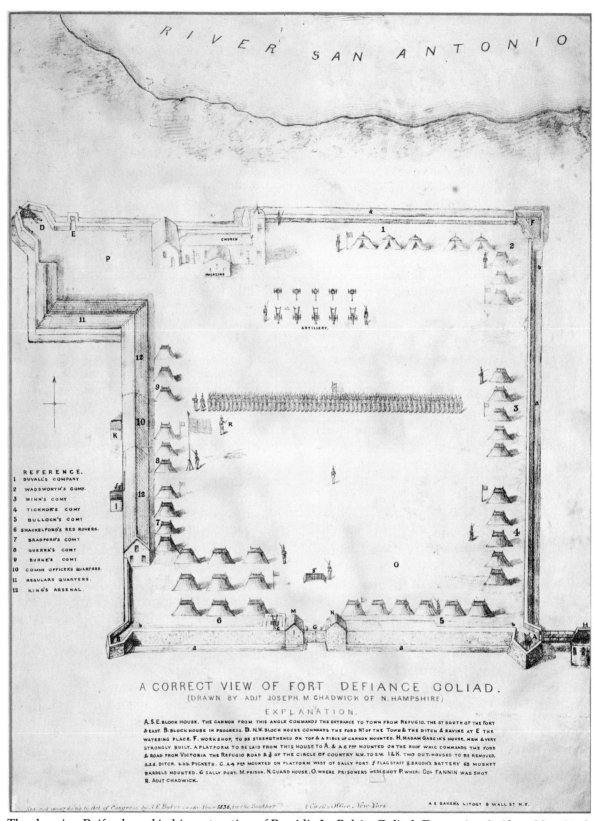

The drawing Raiford used in his restoration of Presidio La Bahía, Goliad. Drawn in 1836 by a New York lithographer, it was based on a smaller drawing made by Capt. Joseph M. Chadwick, adjutant to Colonel Fannin.

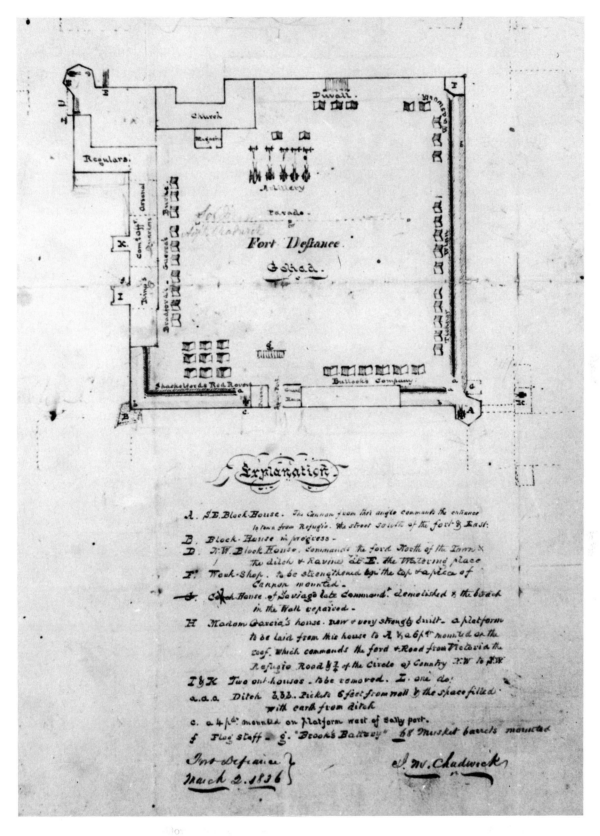

Chadwick's original drawing of the fort at La Bahía. It was found in Charlottesville, Virginia, just after the presidio restoration was completed.

tural historians bemoaned the biases of the movement toward pre-Revolutionary buildings and when the difference between "restoration" and "reconstruction" was first being realized, values and methods had changed. Young architecture students in the late 1960s and early 1970s, fired by the social consciousness of the times, began not only to appreciate Victorian and vernacular architecture but also to distrust the generation of architects that preceded them. After all, who could be more to blame for such sins as urban renewal and the plastering of historic storefronts than practicing architects of the 1950s and 1960s, who had been trained to think that old was bad and new was good? Unfortunately, older Modernists were not the only ones blamed. The generation gap could extend to anyone over thirty—even Raiford Stripling, something of a rebel himself and certainly no proponent of the International Style, who would nevertheless butt heads with the new breed of preservation architect then coming of age.

For one thing, the 1930s love affair with house-museum restorations and reconstructions was fading. Young preservation architects were now talking about "adaptive reuse" and "preservation," the former a practical means of restoring a historic building in order to use it, the latter a more inclusive way to halt the aging process and to honestly highlight the architecture more or less as is, including all the additions and modifications that have themselves become historic. The idea now was to recycle old buildings in an era of dwindling resources and, if at all possible, to protect their "integrity," which meant not only ensuring that they were structurally sound but also preserving their genuine "character," a cumulative blend of style, texture, color, age, use, place, and a kind of craftsmanship that is almost impossible to reproduce. In a revival of Ruskin's nineteenth-century polemic against destroying historic architecture in order to save it, the bywords now

were: don't fake it; don't overdo it; and, if an old building is not structurally sound, potentially useful, or particularly significant, don't restore it.

A good example of this "new" way of appreciating old architecture was the preservation of the Maxey House in Paris, Texas, in 1976 by the Austin firm Bell, Klein, and Hoffman. The significance of the house stemmed not only from its architecture—which is considered an excellent example of the transition from Greek Revival to Victorian—but also from the fact that one family lived in it for almost a hundred years. Descendants of Sam Bell Maxey, Confederate general, lawyer, and U.S. senator, inhabited the house from the time it was built in 1867 to the death of Maxey descendant Sallie Lee Lightfoot in 1966. The family donated the house to the Texas Parks and Wildlife Department, which had set up its own Historic Sites and Restoration Branch a few years before. The department then commissioned Wayne Bell, John Klein, and David Hoffman—who met in the early seventies while working for the branch—to preserve the house as it was in 1966. Although they would have to "restore" it to a certain point in time (1966), the idea was then to preserve ninety-nine years of the house's history as a home. Architects developed a preservation plan "to illustrate not only the historical significance of the architecture but to illuminate the fact that change is part of the natural life of buildings and only increases their worth and interest as historic structures."[7]

As the definition of historical and architectural significance broadened, architects and archaeologists became more conservative in their investigations of building and site. With a renewed appreciation of architectural character and integrity, and always on the alert for the flimsiest thread of evi-

---

[7]Michael McCullar, "Profile: Bell, Klein & Hoffman," *Texas Architect* (January-February, 1982): 33.

dence, architects began to probe ever so gently into the building fabric so as not to damage anything just for the sake of "patriotic education." Archaeologists also dug more gingerly in their excavations to avoid damaging the newer, upper layers of the site, which now were every bit as important as the older, deeper ones.

The movement was also becoming more specialized and scientific. Younger architects were learning how to be "preservation technologists," a new kind of specialist who had the perspective of the historian, the skills of the architect, and the focus of a "conservator." Methods for measuring and documenting with the utmost accuracy came to include such newfangled wizardry as stereophotogrammetry, which measures buildings in three dimensions; rectified photography for recording in two-dimensional images; computers for figuring and drafting; microscopic and chemical analysis of original materials; and portable x-ray systems for examining hidden elements of a building without destroying everything else.

Meanwhile, Raiford was still *restoring* old buildings, and doing so in a kind of seat-of-the-pants way that the younger architects considered outmoded. He still scratched out his college trigonometry on a yellow legal pad—refusing to use even a slide rule, much less a computer—and still relied mainly on his eyes and intuition to determine what was there before. Once considered the idealistic, headstrong purist, Raiford was now running up against an even more demanding school of preservation thought and being challenged, ironically, for being an old-school romanticist.

Philosophical friction between Raiford and the young turks first ignited in 1972, when Parks and Wildlife commissioned him to restore Zaragoza's birthplace in Goliad. Again, Raiford was the logical choice for the job, since he had done so much preservation work there already and had already become something of a "dean" of preservation

architects in Texas. Actually, he was first commissioned to do the job in the late sixties, going so far as to produce a complete set of drawings, but for one reason or another the project was shelved. In 1972, however, when he began working with David Hoffman—then a young apprentice architect right out of UT and working for the Historic Sites and Restoration Branch—Raiford had a hard time doing what he thought was right. At issue was whether the three-room, limestone house was grand or humble in appearance when Mexican general Ignacio Seguin Zaragoza was born in it on March 24, 1829. The son of a Mexican army officer stationed at La Bahía, Zaragoza went on to become one of Mexico's greatest heroes, commanding the Army of the East and routing an invading French force at Puebla on May 5, 1862, a day now celebrated throughout Mexico and in much of Texas as Cinco de Mayo. After studying the original set of drawings, Hoffman could not escape the conclusion that Raiford had taken too many liberties with the project. According to Hoffman, the drawings—based on little more than an existing limestone wall line—portrayed a fairly elaborate abode, complete with painted wainscoting and wrought-iron light fixtures and window grilles. Raiford's scheme also called for leaving the limestone walls exposed, as he did at La Bahía. It was a nice interpretation, Hoffman says, only not very accurate. Hoffman was convinced that the structure was more likely a modest stucco dwelling, typical of the houses that surrounded the presidio and more fitting for a company-grade officer in the Mexican army.

To prove his theory, Hoffman and fellow staff architect John Klein went down to the border and studied indigenous houses of a similar vintage and level of sophistication as Zaragoza's birthplace. Combining their research with archaeological investigations that the department had done—which indicated that floors had been of swept earth and the detailing fairly simple—Hoffman presented their findings to Raiford, who agreed to redraw and supervise the project. Throughout, however (as he remains to this day), Raiford was convinced that his original interpretation was perfectly valid. "It was one of those things that kinda rankled me," he says, "in that I knew Zaragoza's mother was from a family of means" and could have afforded to build a home as elaborate as the presidio. Raiford also points out that the house was built in a prominent spot—just across the street from the presidio—and by the time it was built there were plenty of artisans and craftsmen in Goliad who had worked on the presidio and who could have created the same kind of detailing on the house. In spite of Raiford's misgivings about the revised scheme, Hoffman says, Raiford was cooperative throughout the project, but Hoffman could tell that the old maestro's heart wasn't in it and that he probably thought Hoffman and Klein were just a couple of pedantic whippersnappers who had a hell of a lot to learn about historic preservation.

Nor has Raiford always seen eye-to-eye with Hoffman and Klein's partner in Austin, Wayne Bell, another of the state's leading preservation architects who has been largely responsible for restoring the wealth of historic Texas homes at Winedale—many of which, Raiford says, are painted in colors that have no basis in historical fact. Raiford's aversion to Victorian paint—just about anything other than Greek Revival white or the natural colors of limestone and log—intensified during his own restoration of French's Trading Post in Beaumont. "Those women had all been to the Winedale conference and they wanted to put some blue on the trim on the house," Raiford says. "I took out my pocketknife and went around and showed them some of the original trim. I'd scratch it all the way back to the wood—there was never any blue paint on there." Raiford told his clients, "Long as I'm super-

vising it, there's not gonna be any blue paint on it. Now, after I leave, if y'all want to paint it blue, I can't do anything about it." Raiford rises in his chair with the memory, "And by god that's what they *did*!"

Architects and historians with the Historical Commission had similar run-ins with Raiford. Peter Maxon, director of survey and registration in the THC's national registry department, gives Raiford a lot of credit for raising public awareness of historic preservation in the 1930s—along with San Antonio architects O'Neil Ford, Harvey P. Smith, and Robert H. H. Hugman—and is aware of the generation gap that cracks open from time to time in the ever-evolving field of preservation. But there is one thing that stands out in his mind that is indicative of a somewhat contentious relationship between Raiford and the Historical Commission: Raiford once made a presentation to a THC conference on preservation technology, Maxon says, at a time when reverence for original fabric was on the rise and the traditional method of sandblasting to remove paint from masonry walls was becoming anathema to the movement. With typically sly irreverence, Raiford told the conferees to go ahead and sandblast—just make sure they did it carefully, with the proper tools and techniques, and when the Commission wasn't looking.

As the preservation movement began to place more emphasis on preservation than restoration, another of Raiford's projects—Independence Hall at Washington-on-the-Brazos—came to exemplify the uncertainty of historic reconstruction (see chapter 6). Raiford began the $45,000 project for the state Building Commission in the summer of 1969, charged with building a structure that looked exactly like the original did when the Texas Declaration of Independence was signed on March 2, 1836. To that end, Raiford spent months looking for documents and photographs to add to the exhaustive research that project historian

R. Henderson Shuffler had already conducted. But the more information that was found, it seemed, the more it conflicted. By the time it burned to the ground sometime before the turn of the century, the small frame building had been remodeled numerous times to suit a variety of uses, and even though it stood for some fifty years as a well-known landmark—during a time when photography was becoming fairly common—there was no reliable evidence of what it looked like. Excited by the project, Raiford went on to create a reasonable replication of the building, based on the scholarly findings of Shuffler and a team of archaeologists as well as his own research and intuitions. As Shuffler wrote for the *Southwestern Historical Quarterly* in 1962, however, referring to the annual hoopla surrounding the anniversary of the declaration signing (which he was convinced didn't occur until March 3), "The height of emotion with which this anniversary is observed is matched only by the depth of ignorance about the original event and about the surroundings in which it occurred."[8] Seven years later, the fact remained that there was really no way to tell for sure what Independence Hall looked like in March of 1836, and Shuffler's skepticism is still shared by some archaeologists and historians who are familiar with the project.

As values and methods continued to change, it eventually became clear to second-generation preservationists in the field that no matter how thorough their investigations are, no one can claim to have done an absolutely pure restoration. What Raiford did with Independence Hall was to create a representation of what very well could have been, in the finest tradition of "patriotic education." After all, something had to be built for the public to get an idea of where

the Texas Declaration of Independence was signed. It was a position in which Raiford would often find himself, caught between the pressures of his preservation-group client to get something built and the scrutiny of state agencies like the Historical Commission, which is staffed with historians and archaeologists who can be very picky about such things as sparing historic fabric and documenting visions of how a building might have looked. Even the public was becoming harder to please. The architect could follow the restoration or reconstruction program to a tee, relying on the most comprehensive research and analysis to create the most exact likeness of the original building that was humanly possible, and there was still no guarantee that the project would be a success.

No one knows this phenomenon better than David Hoffman. A hard-charging neophyte in 1972, Hoffman was in awe of Raiford and his wealth of experience in preservation. And it was difficult for him to lock horns with such a venerable institution, whom Hoffman came to respect as he would a historic building. Particularly memorable for the young preservationist were the monthly inspections Raiford would conduct down in Goliad, in which he would "command the site" in a way that architects just don't do anymore, able to speak the working man's language without letting him forget who the boss was. Hoffman also remembers visiting Raiford at his office in the Blount House in San Augustine and marveling at the *analytiques* from Raiford's college days hanging on the walls. But facts were facts, and Hoffman could not understand how Raiford could base his interpretations on such "weak" methodology. In Raiford's original scheme for Zaragoza's birthplace, Hoffman says, it was as if he simply thought that a variation on the Spanish Governor's Palace in San Antonio "would be nice," if not academically sound. The more Hoffman practiced, however, the more he realized

---

[8] R. Henderson Shuffler, "The Signing of Texas' Declaration of Independence: Myth and Record," *Southwestern Historical Quarterly* 65 (July, 1961–April, 1962): 310.

how inexact the science of historic preservation really is. The Maxey House project, which looked upon the house as more than just a work of architecture built at a specific point in time, considerably softened Hoffman's hard-core, purist approach. Then came the commission to restore the Sam Houston Home in Huntsville in 1979, which Hoffman says made him "grow up a lot."

The Sam Houston restoration was a landmark project in the evolution of historic preservation in Texas, in part because it went against the direction of the movement. By the late 1970s, the trend away from restoring and rebuilding house museums and toward preserving and recycling useful buildings had been given great impetus by the Tax Reform Act of 1976. This act allowed owners of historic properties to amortize the costs of building rehabilitation over a five-year period and to depreciate the adjusted basis of the rehabilitated property (the cost of the building plus capital improvements and less depreciation) at a faster rate than normal, as long as rehabilitation costs exceeded five thousand dollars, or the adjusted basis. The 1976 tax act was amended by the Economic Recovery Tax Act of 1981, which provided even more financial incentives for historic preservation, including a "three-tiered" investment tax credit. Building owners could get a 15 percent deduction from their taxes for rehabilitating income-producing properties at least thirty years old, 20 percent for structures at least forty years old, and 25 percent for "certified historic structures" (residential and nonresidential buildings listed on the National Register of Historic Places or located in, and contributing to the significance of, a Registered Historic District). No tax credit was allowed for buildings less than thirty years old, unless they were certified historic structures. (At this writing, these financial incentives are threatened by the Reagan administration's proposed tax reform plan, which would eliminate the tax

credits for restoring historic buildings and quite possibly result in a dramatic setback for the preservation movement.)

The result was a whirlwind of activity all across the country, in downtowns big and small. Ornate Victorian storefronts that had been plastered for decades—especially in economically dormant cities like Austin, Fort Worth, and Galveston, where there was still a lot of historic building stock— were being restored with the utmost attention to period detail, their insides gutted and remade to serve modern purposes. The National Trust also initiated its highly successful Main Street Program in 1977, for which Texas was chosen as a participating state in 1980. The essence of the Main Street strategy, administered on the state level in Texas by the THC, is to persuade small-town banks and savings and loans to provide merchants with low-interest loans so they can restore the historic facades of their buildings and otherwise improve their storefront merchandising. Rather than look at economic vitality and historic preservation as being mutually exclusive, Main Street is designed to achieve both—create more business downtown by beautifying old architecture.

Meanwhile, the Board of Regents at Sam Houston State University in Huntsville commissioned Bell, Klein, and Hoffman to restore the Sam Houston Home, a prim white-clapboard dogtrot with a Greek Revival portico and both a National Register Landmark and a Recorded Texas State Historic Landmark. It was a classic house-museum commission; using all available evidence, architects were to return the house precisely to the point in time when Sam Houston lived there in the 1850s. Following the client's program to the letter, the firm proceeded to uncover and restore original wall timbers, covering cracks in between with horizontal battens and whitewashing the exterior. Architects also removed the gabled front portico and rebuilt a rear porch and some rooms that were once attached to the back. Although no old photograph could be found showing Houston himself sitting on the front porch, the weight of evidence indicated that it was a far simpler house in the 1850s than it appeared to be in 1979. Preservationists with the Walker County Historical Commission, who had grown accustomed to the historic house as a clapboard dogtrot with Greek Revival portico, vehemently disagreed with that interpretation—so much so that they took regents and architects to court. A Huntsville judge issued a restraining order to halt work on the project and ruled that the Historical Commission's Antiquities Committee would have to approve the changes, which it did. After much publicity and litigation, the courts finally ruled in favor of the $175,000 project, which was completed in 1982.

Hoffman came out of the experience with a greater appreciation of how history is perceived and a greater understanding of Raiford's approach to preservation. Controversy surrounding the restoration of the Sam Houston Home showed that the preservation movement had finally reached a point where historical accuracy at all costs was no longer a completely valid approach. Well aware of the differences between restoration and preservation going into the project, Hoffman came to appreciate the fact that historical and architectural significance, like beauty, is very much in the eye of the beholder. What people have grown accustomed to viewing as historic can often be as "real" as any scholarly interpretation—perhaps even more so. Although the facades of many of the Spanish missions were at some point painted with colorful patterns resembling Moorish tiles, no mission restoration in Texas has attempted to re-create that (save for a small portion of the church wall at San José, where San Antonio artist Ernst Schuchard reproduced an original motif of red and blue quatrefoils back in the 1930s). What Raiford elected to do in Go-

liad, he says, was to "put it there, and not try to interpret it for anybody. . . . Tell 'em what it is, then let them figure it out." As Hoffman says, "Raiford would always draw the line, then beyond that he felt free to romanticize a bit. The more I practice, the more I understand that." No matter what, as Hoffman's wife (and firm historian) Binnie Hoffman says, "it is still all conjecture."

Raggy Stripling graduated from A&M in 1966 with a degree in architectural engineering and, after working for construction companies in Dallas and Kentucky, returned to San Augustine in 1969 with his wife and nine-month-old daughter to live in the Blount House and practice architecture with his dad. Raiford had been trying to get his son to join him since Raggy graduated from A&M, but, like his father, Raggy was very much his own man and determined to make his way. It wasn't long, however, before he realized that working for a big construction company wasn't his cup of tea. Although he considered himself something of a city boy when he lived in Victoria, and he probably could have made more money in Dallas, Raggy came to realize that the pace and anonymity of urban life appealed to him far less than the simple small-town pleasures of life in San Augustine.

After the birth of Raiford's second granddaughter in 1970, it wasn't long before the Blount House got to be a little cramped as a place to live and work. So Raiford talked his father into taking some money that Raif had just made by selling some downtown property and using it to fix up the old jail, which Raif had owned since the 1920s when the "new" jail was built next to Shirley Simons's courthouse. The old jail hadn't been used for years for anything other than storing seed and dynamite (iron bars were ripped out of the windows of the old jail and reused on the new one). It was not meticulously restored—only refurbished a bit. New windows were installed, floors redone, partitions put up, and walls painted, then Raiford and Raggy moved their office to the top floor, leaving the bottom floor for reception and storage.

Raiford and Raggy have gotten along quite well as partners in their firm Raiford Stripling Associates, a relationship no doubt enhanced by the fact that Raggy shares Raiford's love for the Greek Revival, believing that (as most things classical tend to do) "it stands the test of time." Their thirty-six-bed Sabine County Hospital in Hemphill, completed in 1980, features an assortment of Greek Revival details you don't often find on rural county hospitals (see chapter 6). Their partnership has also been good because of Raggy's continuing admiration for his father. In the tradition of the Beaux Arts *charette*, Raiford has often amazed his son—who considers himself a more methodical, plodding practitioner— with an uncanny ability to sit down at his drawing board with his pencils and cigarettes, tune out the world, and do a complete set of drawings in a day and a half.

While Raiford takes up the slack in the production department, Raggy looks after the money. In some ways, their working relationship is reminiscent of Vosper and Raiford's in the thirties, when Vosper concentrated on his art·and Raiford took care of all the business. Raiford is the eternal optimist, Raggy says, never worrying about where the money is going to come from, perfectly content as long as he has enough for food, Marlboros, and shotgun shells. (During his Waco restorations in the 1950s and 1960s [see chapter 6], Raiford won the hearts of Waco preservationists in part because of his generosity. According to Lavonia Jenkins Barnes, the "mother of restoration" in Waco, Raiford saw fit to restore the Earle-Harrison House free of charge. With his other three Waco projects, she says, Raiford would never give her a fixed price for his services up front, remaining flexible with his fee throughout the project. "You never know how much rotten wood you're going to find," he would tell her. And when he

did agree on something, she says, Raiford always held to his word.) And as long as they have practiced together, Raggy says, Raiford has never competed with other architects for work; most of it comes to him, in part because of Raiford's reputation as a designer and preservationist and in part because of his ability to "command the site." The firm prides itself on job supervision, never taking any kind of commission unless Raiford or Raggy can be there when the work is done. In explaining the division of their responsibilities, Raiford likes to say that whoever is in the office when the phone rings is "Leroy," but the fact is that Raggy is Leroy when it comes to managing the practice, Raiford is Leroy when it comes to design, and both are Leroy on the job site.

Raggy assumed the business responsibilities of the firm not only because of their respective inclinations but also because of Raiford's health. He had developed diabetes in the mid-1960s, when he gave up drinking for good, telling his doctor, "You'll never treat me for that again." Moving out to the Garrett House to live full-time in 1979, after his mother died (for years she worried about her diabetic son living alone in the country), Raiford continued to fight temptation valiantly and successfully—even though for the first time in his life he lived within walking distance of a liquor store. It wouldn't have done him much good anyway, for he got to where he couldn't walk a hundred yards without intense pain in his legs, which the doctors attributed to arthritis and poor circulation and which effectively put a halt to his quail hunting.

And as important as his eyes were to his work, it was especially unfortunate when, in 1979, Raiford suffered a detached retina in one eye and cataracts in both eyes. He had worn glasses since he was a kid, but the strain of the drawing board and the intensity of his work-hard–play-hard way of life were finally catching up with him. For two years thereafter, Raiford couldn't draw so much as a line with a pencil, much less a

Mission Espíritu Santo, Goliad. (Photograph by J. Griffis Smith)

Rear view of Mission Espíritu Santo, Goliad. (Photograph by J. Griffis Smith)

Presidio La Bahía and grounds, Goliad. (Photograph by J. Griffis Smith)

Raiford's watercolor rendering of the chapel at Presidio La Bahía, Goliad.

Interior of the chapel at Presidio La Bahía, Goliad. (Photograph by J. Griffis Smith)

Rear view of Presidio La Bahía, Goliad. (Photograph by J. Griffis Smith)

The well at Presidio La Bahía, Goliad. (Photograph by J. Griffis Smith)

Earle-Harrison House, Waco. (Photograph by J. Griffis Smith)

Earle-Napier-Kinnard House, Waco. (Photograph by J. Griffis Smith)

Ashton Villa, Galveston. (Photographs by J. Griffis Smith)

Parlor, Ashton Villa, Galveston. (Photograph by J. Griffis Smith)

Hall and stairway, Ashton Villa, Galveston. (Photograph by J. Griffis Smith)

Independence Hall, Washington-on-the-Brazos. (Photograph by J. Griffis Smith)

Sabine County Hospital, Hemphill. (Photograph by Laura Cicarella)

bead with a shotgun, so he hardly practiced or hunted at all. He grew despondent, needless to say, his spirits buoyed only by the affections of his granddaughters. Throughout the ordeal, Raggy says, Raiford was never a very good patient; he was always too proud and independent to ask anybody to do anything for him. Once, when Raiford had an appointment in Lufkin with his ophthalmologist, Dr. Thomas Duncan, he insisted upon driving there and back himself. He had gotten to where he could drive pretty well by then, Raggy says, but not with his pupils dilated. Raggy offered to take him, but Raiford declined, and the next thing Raggy knew, Raiford had miraculously made it all the way back from Lufkin without incident—until he pulled into the office parking lot and rammed into the side of Raggy's pickup.

After a lens implant in both eyes in 1982, Raiford's eyesight slowly improved, and so did his spirits. He even allowed Raggy to take him to the doctor to be fitted for his final pair of new glasses, and all the way there they talked about how his eyesight would never be as good as it was and how he shouldn't get his hopes up. Raggy dropped him off at the doctor's office, and when he returned to pick him up, Raiford was beside himself, looking around excitedly and saying, "Man, I'm seeing things I haven't seen since I was fifteen years old."

Raiford returned to work in January of 1983, easing into it at first, then getting back into the swing of things as though he had never left. Staying as busy as he liked, Raiford always seemed to have a couple of preservation projects going somewhere, but in recent years, particularly during the Houston boom, most of the firm's work has been residential—"Neo-Greek Revival" houses perched on hills around the lakes for retirees from Houston, Lufkin, Tyler, and Nacogdoches. They seek Raiford out, as O'Neil Ford was sought out in his golden emeritus years, not as a preservationist but as a regionalist—a "name" architect who is

a homegrown Texan and whose touch will lend real value as well as quality to a home.

Still living in San Augustine and being the oldest boy, Raiford has assumed more and more of the family leadership as he has turned over more and more of the firm's leadership to Raggy. One of Raiford's most regular responsibilities is helping to oversee Stripling's Drugstore, which his youngest sister Mary Jane continues to run but which hasn't been a real pharmacy since their father died. It is now more of a luncheonette than anything else, with Mary Jane behind the counter serving up hamburgers and sandwiches. And every day he's in town, Raiford walks to the drugstore for lunch, where he usually sits at the counter and does more talking than eating as people he has known all his life drop in and stop to grab his arm and chat as they walk to their tables. The drugstore is also something of a museum. To the left of the lunch counter is an old well, dug by slaves in 1860 and restored a hundred years later as a town landmark. On the wall above the well are photographs of Striplings, going all the way back to Raiford's grandfather, and upstairs all sorts of relics are displayed—strands of barbed wire, pioneer dresses, antique furniture, old medicine bottles, and drugstore ledgers.

Raiford goes so far as to extend his filial responsibilities to those outside his family and race (as Southerners often do, even as the word "nigger" rolls off his tongue with ease and regularity). At least once a week he will look in on Peter Payne and his wife Rawsie over in the "black quarter," where they live in a small, clapboard bungalow Peter built in 1932. "If either of us takes sick," Peter says, "he or Raggy either one will carry us to the doctor's office." And if they have business in town that Peter may not understand, Rawsie says, Raiford or Raggy will explain things to Peter and make sure no one takes advantage of the old man.

Raiford was also the instigator of a Stripling family tradition that was thoroughly enjoyed by all until Raif and Winfrey died, after which it was never quite the same. Every Christmas after Raiford fixed up the Garrett House, he would host a "bird supper" in it, usually quail or dove that he had killed during hunting season. Everyone would attend: Robert and his family from Midland (where Robert had done rather well in the oil business since leaving Washington in the late forties), Frances and Martha and their families from Dallas. All told, counting nieces and nephews, as many as thirty-five quail eaters would descend upon the Garrett House, says Robert, who remembers how fires would blaze in both fireplaces, one on each end of the house, and how their father would take the opportunity to consume the only alcohol he consumed all year—two beers. One year, Robert remembers, Minor Morgan, the ten-year-old son of sister Sarah (who died of cancer in the mid-1970s), came into the kitchen where Raiford was serving and held out his plate. "Boy, I can't afford you," Raiford said. "You've eaten *nine* birds already!" With that, Raiford reached into a kitchen cabinet, pulled out a can of sardines, and handed it to Minor. "Finish up on these," he said. "Those birds are too precious for your inflated ap-pe-*tite*."

As if to validate Raiford's diehard faith in classical architecture, contemporary design has moved into a kind of transitional phase called, for lack of a better term, "Post-Modernism," which respectfully looks to the past again for inspiration. According to architectural historian Charles Jencks, this stylistic historicism was first hinted at in America in the medieval walkways, massing, and stonework of Eero Saarinen's work at Yale in the late 1950s and early 1960s.[9] Ironically, one of the most articulate and prolific spokesmen for this new "movement" turned out to be Philip Johnson, who

helped coin the term International Style back in the thirties. By the early sixties, Johnson had lost his love for glass-box Miesian Modernism and was urging a return to traditions in architecture that were eclectic and ornamental. Mies's dictum "Less is more" would be countered with "Less is a bore." Johnson realized that it was impossible to ignore the influence of the past, an awareness that manifested itself in his Amon Carter Museum in Fort Worth, built in 1961 and featuring such un-Modern elements as the segmental arch. "We cannot not know history," Johnson once said.[10]

Later, Philadelphia architect Robert Venturi became a Post-Modern standard-bearer with his classic polemic against Modernism, *Complexity and Contradiction in Architecture*, published by the Museum of Modern Art in New York in 1966. In it he argued for an all-embracing approach to design that would be complex rather than simple, hybrid rather than pure, messy rather than clean. By the late seventies, architects were rejecting the machine as an exclusive metaphor for design and evoking more and more of the past in bigger and bigger buildings, designing in a vein that *New York Times* architecture critic Paul Goldberger has come to call Romantic Modernism—a blend of Modern sleekness and materials with the more sculptural and decorative forms of Post-Modernism.[11] (Goldberger has also noted a return to a kind of "pure restoration" in which the original function as well as integrity of a historic building is preserved—when an atrociously renovated Beaux Arts library, for example, is recycled into a "new" Beaux Arts library instead of a fern bar.)[12]

Two notable examples of this Romantic Modernism, both designed by Philip

[9]Charles Jencks, *The Language of Post-Modern Architecture* (New York: Rizzoli International, 1980), p. 82.

[10]Ibid.
[11]Paul Goldberger, "Romantic Modernism Is Now at the Cutting Edge of Design," *New York Times*, July 9, 1984.
[12]Paul Goldberger, "Preserving the Original Function as Well as Detail Is Key to Today's Restoration," *New York Times Magazine*, October 7, 1984, p. 55.

Johnson and his partner John Burgee, do much to accentuate the dazzling skyline in Houston: RepublicBank, with its Gothic spires and pinnacles, and Transco Tower, with its ribs and setbacks so reminiscent of the great Art Deco skyscrapers built in the 1920s and 1930s. And as proof of the fact that architectural appreciation is in a continuous state of flux, even some of those plastered facades that preservationists have been bemoaning and ripping off for years are now being preserved. The Vogue, a 1950s shoe shop turned restaurant on historic Congress Avenue in downtown Austin and recently restored by Austin architects Robert Smith and Tom Lea, sits proudly among an array of restored Victorian storefronts, its smooth marble, glass, and neon facade adding to the time line of Austin's architecture.

Vascular surgery in July of 1984 to improve the circulation in his legs has helped his walking considerably, and Raiford is returning to the field to hunt quail—something he has been unable to do for years without a great deal of discomfort. He also continues to enjoy *columbarie* (hand-thrown) pigeon shoots, festive affairs sponsored by the Tiro al Pichon Association in San Antonio and held throughout the South and West in the spring and summer so that avid bird hunters will have something to do in the off-season. Raiford says that bird hunting in San Augustine County hasn't been very good anyway since the U.S. Department of Agriculture started its pasture-improvement program some ten or fifteen years ago, clearing away an awful lot of cover and food.

Raiford made one of his most desperate attempts to preserve the purity of his place in the sixties, when the big lakes were being built on either side of San Augustine County—Sam Rayburn to the southwest and Toledo Bend to the east. There were still a lot of old houses scattered about then, and Raiford went around trying to find and buy as many as he could before the waters rose.

He succeeded only in buying the Garrett House, which wasn't even threatened by the dams, but he still has his eye on the old Scurlock House over in Sabine County, a story-and-a-half frame house with a stick-and-mud chimney and a delicate dab of Greek Revival millwork. Raiford says he's negotiating with two elderly women to buy the house and move it to a place on Patroon Creek, which feeds into Toledo Bend, where he can sit on the front porch and fish or shoot ducks.

Meanwhile, as he grows more vigorous by the day, rebounding from vascular surgery much as he did from eye surgery, Raiford has no desire to spend his time in a kind of nomadic retirement, traveling outside the state just to tour and sightsee. Although he would like to get back to Washington someday, Raiford chooses to invest his new-won vigor in his work and play, doing what he has always wanted to do more than anything else: practice architecture and hunt birds. Nevertheless, Raiford is growing old, becoming more and more like Vosper in some ways—and in other ways like one of his beloved bird dogs. As his old hunting buddy Peter Payne says, of the two breeds he has trained the most—pointers and setters—he likes the pointer best. He is sleek and fast and tries the hardest to please, but he is so fast that his legs wear out before his heart does, and his working life is rarely longer than twelve years or so. "The old setter, he got a slow lope, and I don't care what you say, he just goin' to keep that up. But an old pointer, when you turn him loose, he just like lightnin'—over here and over there. But he'll lose his nose and his way runnin' before long, and get to be like an old man."

More than anything else, Raiford is fixed to his Deep East Texas habitat by instinct, and by certain stirrings and sounds that only he can make out. "Usually a covey of quail will be calling me somewhere," he says. "I hear those birds better than I hear anybody else."

CHAPTER 6

Projects

Restoration of the Earle-Harrison House, Earle-Napier-Kinnard House,
Fort House, and East Terrace, Waco

Raiford has never determined who actually built the four homes he restored here—the Augustus Phelps or Abner Cook of Waco—but he still sings the praises of their craftsmanship, which no doubt was enhanced by pattern books of the day showing them how to produce fluted columns and laminated wood capitals. Raiford is also fond of saying how much he enjoyed "spendin' all that cotton money."

A lot can be said, of course, for the prosperity of the times and the tastes of the people who contributed to and benefited by it. The town of Waco was laid out in 1849, named after an Indian tribe in the area, and by the mid-fifties it was already making the transition from frontier settlement to boomtown, its prosperity based on the ascendance of King Cotton. People drawn to the area, as Raiford writes in the foreword to *Early Homes of Waco* by Lavonia Jenkins Barnes, came largely from the Old South and "had the perseverance and endurance required to bring a measure of style and culture to the Texas frontier."[1]

One of the first Waco immigrants to really take advantage of the black Brazos River bottomland around Waco was Dr. Baylis Wood Earle, a South Carolina native and the son of a general in the Revolutionary army. After receiving his medical degree from Transylvania College in Kentucky, Dr. Earle practiced medicine with his brother in Alabama, then in 1833 moved with his wife and three children to Aberdeen, Mississippi, where he prospered as a planter as well as a physician.

His son, John Baylis Earle, moved to Waco in 1855 and, presumably, imparted his enthusiasm about the area in letters to Dr. Earle, who soon began buying up large tracts of land in and around Waco—1,280 acres east of the Brazos River, 1,000 acres on the west side, and one and one-fourth acres between South Fourth and South Fifth streets on which to build a home.

Dr. and Mrs. Earle moved with their two other children to Waco in 1857 or 1858, and work on their house began shortly thereafter, probably being completed in 1859. Unlike later homes built in Waco after the brick kilns began operating, the Earle-Harrison House was constructed of wood, much of which was brought in from the

[1] Raiford Stripling, foreword to *Early Homes of Waco and the People Who Lived in Them*, by Lavonia Jenkins Barnes (Waco: Texian Press, 1981), p. vii.

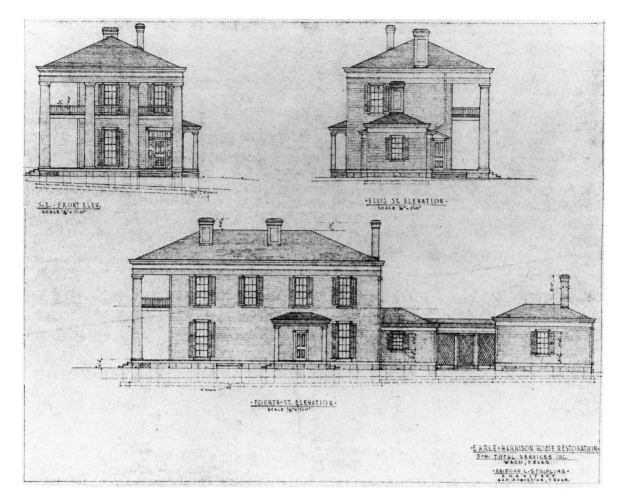

Raiford's drawings of the elevations for the Earle-Harrison House in Waco.

coast—cypress siding, heart-of-pine flooring. In all probability, the heavy post-oak framing came from a nearby grove, and brick for the chimneys was made on site by Dr. Earle's slaves.

It is one of the finest Greek Revival houses in the state—two stories in height, painted white, with an entablature and upper gallery supported by nine-inch-thick Doric columns wrapping across its front and around the south side. Each room opens onto the lower or upper gallery by windows tall enough to walk through. And it could have been designed to be even more classical. Raiford is convinced that only half the house was built. The hipped roof and

the doweled corners on the north side suggest that the original design called for a peristyle structure—one with equal portions on either side of a central hallway and surrounded by a colonnade, like a classic Greek temple. Raiford also theorizes that its builder was a shipwright—not uncommon in those days—since some of the timbers are fitted together rather than nailed.

Sometime after the Civil War, the house was bought by a local lawyer and war hero, Gen. Thomas Harrison. The general was born in Alabama, studied law in Mississippi, and in 1843 moved to Brazoria, Texas, to practice with his brother. After his brother died, he returned to Mississippi, where in

Doric columns supporting the upper gallery and entablature of the Earle-Harrison House, Waco. (Photograph by J. Griffis Smith)

1846 he enlisted in the First Mississippi Rifles, under the command of Col. Jefferson Davis, and fought in the Mexican War. When that was over he returned to Texas and in 1850 was elected to the state legislature. During the Civil War, he organized a company of cavalry in Waco that eventually became part of Terry's Rangers, an illustrious Confederate outfit, and rose to the rank of brigadier general, distinguishing himself at the battles of Shiloh and Murfreesboro.

After the war, the general returned to Waco and purchased the mansion from his sister Mrs. Earle, whose husband had died in 1859. The general added a kitchen (origi-

nally detached) to the main part of the house, the whole of which he moved to the edge of the property on the South Fourth Street side in 1872. A sketch of the Earle-Harrison House, at that time still one of the grandest homes in Waco, appeared in the September 27, 1891, issue of Frank Leslie's *Illustrated Weekly*.

Unfortunately, the house did not fare so well in twentieth-century Waco; it was divided into apartments during World War II, as Raiford says, "and really messed up." It was practically in ruins in 1968, when Mrs. G. H. Pape told Lavonia Barnes that she would pay for the restoration of any old house in Waco that Lavonia considered

Tall window opening onto a lower gallery, Earle-Harrison House, Waco. (Photograph by J. Griffis Smith)

worthy of salvation. In part because it was one of the only two antebellum houses still standing in Waco, Lavonia chose the Earle-Harrison House, which its owner—Citizens National Bank—donated to the G. H. Pape Foundation.

Lavonia then commissioned Raiford to restore the house, services he too would donate to the cause, but that didn't mean the project would be easy. Before any restoration could begin, the house had to be moved, so Raiford hired a house mover, who dismantled all the brick chimneys, removed the roof and columns, cut the studs, and laid the walls of the second floor down on top of the first floor. Then on Labor Day, 1968, the house was transported thirty-four blocks across town. And because of its heavy post-oak framing, Raiford says, it was a "helluva load to move."

After reassembling the house on its new site on North Fifth Street, Raiford scraped all the cypress and pine siding down, repainted it, rebuilt a replica of the original detached kitchen on the west side of the house, refinished the woodwork, repapered the walls, and took out all the dropped ceilings and apartment partitions. Completely refurnished with period pieces, the house is now maintained and operated by the G. H. Pape Foundation as a house museum, is open to the public by appointment, and may be rented for "suitable occasions."

The Earle-Napier-Kinnard House, Waco. (Photograph by J. Griffis Smith)

The Earle-Napier-Kinnard House on South Fourth Street started out as a two-room brick dwelling, built around 1858 by Dr. Earle's son John Baylis Earle, who was the first of the family to come to Waco and who sold his father on its potential as a place to live and raise cotton.

Earle sold the house in 1868 to H. S. Morgan, who in turn sold it to John S. Napier that same year. Napier was a well-to-do immigrant from Alabama who moved to Waco shortly after he bought the house, which he proceeded to expand by moving the east wall out three feet, thereby enlarging the dining room, and building a two-story addition onto the west side (work that the Morgans probably started). Napier's

changes made for a somewhat awkward circulation pattern, since he failed to cut a passageway from the one-story original to the two-story addition, making it necessary to go around one end of the open latticed porch to get from one to the other. The porch was eventually enclosed and made into the "tea room," and the original part of the house would serve as the kitchen.

Masonry used for both phases of construction is pink, sandy brick made on the premises and typical of the locally produced brick used to construct many buildings in Waco and three of the four houses that Raiford restored here. The two-story front portico, braced by four fluted Ionic columns, features an ornamental wooden

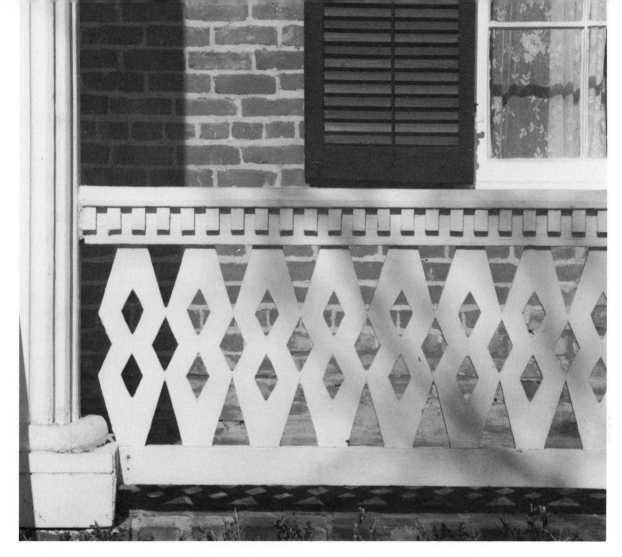

Profiled balusters on the balustrade of the Earle-Napier-Kinnard House, Waco. (Photograph by J. Griffis Smith)

balustrade on both upper and lower galleries. The balusters are "profiled," Raiford emphasizes, cut rough and hand planed—not lathed—out of five-quarter pine (and possibly patterned after a kind of ornamental cast-iron baluster then common in the South). The Ionic capitals were "built up" (laminated) with one-inch pieces of pine and cypress. Other nice touches are the red-cedar lintels, cypress shutters, and sheet-metal leader heads (the enlarged connection between gutter and downspout), which Raiford says was a sure sign of a homeowner's affluence.

Inside, all woodwork was painted white except the doors, stairway, and two man-tels, one of which was finished in "false grain," the other marbleized, a fairly common practice in those days that involved swirling streaks of white paint with a turkey feather onto wood painted a kind of dark green, then varnishing the wood to make it shine like verde marble. Plaster walls throughout the house were whitewashed, save for those in the dining room, which were papered.

Sometime in the late 1870s or early 1880s, the house became the home of the Reverend David Cannon Kinnard and family. Kinnard was a Tennessee native who graduated from Cumberland University in Lebanon, Tennessee, in 1863. During the Civil War he served as a chaplain in an Alabama regiment and afterwards married John Napier's daughter Sallie. In 1869 or 1870, the Kinnards followed the Napiers to Waco, where the reverend eventually became pastor of the Cumberland Presbyterian Church and also developed a reputation as a Greek and Hebrew scholar.

In 1959, the house was bought from Napier descendants by Mrs. George Nalle of Austin, a former Waco resident, who commissioned Raiford to restore it. First he enclosed an open back porch, putting in two bathrooms and two dressing rooms above it, and then he started working on the brick. As in all three of the masonry houses that Raiford restored in Waco, the sandy pink brick used to build the Earle-Napier-Kinnard House was soft and absorbent and therefore hadn't weathered very well over the years. The brick would absorb water, which would freeze in winter and cause the brick to flake off in layers when it thawed. So a lot of the work involved matching and replacing deteriorated brick, repointing the joints, and covering the brick with a colorless waterproofing. Exterior and interior woodwork was also repaired and repainted, and a small portion of the original English wallpaper in the dining room was saved. Raiford also solved a problem that he says is the bane of a Greek Revival restorationist: pigeon droppings on the white cornice and columns, which he guarded against by putting nails on the cornice to keep pigeons from lighting there.

Mrs. Nalle not only bought and had the house restored, she also furnished it with period pieces, set up an endowment for its upkeep, and presented it to the Waco Perpetual Growth Society in 1967. It is now listed on the National Register of Historic Places and is owned by the Historic Waco Foundation, which maintains and operates it as a house museum, open to the public on the weekends from 2:00 to 5:00 P.M. and on other days by appointment.

Built-up Ionic capital, Earle-Napier-Kinnard House, Waco. (Photograph by J. Griffis Smith)

The first post–Civil War house Raiford restored in Waco was the Fort House, another unique example of the Greek Revival in that it shows how the style lagged on its way from East to West. The Greek Revival is generally considered to have never regained its popularity after the Civil War, having been replaced by the refreshingly unabashed styles of the Victorian era. On the western boundary of the Old South, however, Waco was still a distant outpost as far as fashion was concerned, and styles that had died in the East by the late 1860s were still very much alive here.

Fort House, Waco. (Photograph by J. Griffis Smith)

The house was built in 1868 by Col. William Aldredge Fort, a native of La Grange, Alabama, who graduated from La Grange College in 1846 and began a successful career as an Alabama planter and businessman. Visiting Waco in 1854 after having heard so much about its prime farmland, he talked his business partner into moving there with him and a number of other settlers and bought a plantation on the Brazos River four miles south of town. In 1856 he married Dionitia Elizabeth Wilson, who managed the plantation while he was away fighting for the Confederacy. When he returned from the war, during which he rose to the rank of colonel, he soon realized the effects that emancipated labor would have on farming in the area and wisely decided to go into business again, opening a private bank in 1869 that eventually became the First National Bank of Waco.

The house he built in 1868 on the southwest corner of Webster and South Fourth Streets, on a plot of land he bought from his wife, is made of the same sandy pink brick as the Earle-Napier-Kinnard House and features the same kind of two-story, fluted Ionic columns (suggesting that both houses may have been built by the same man). But there are differences. For example, Colonel Fort's house has a four-column portico, whereas the Earle-Napier-Kinnard House has only a two-column one, which is topped with a classic Greek pediment. It is said that the cypress columns were made in New Orleans, shipped to Galveston, then transported to Waco via oxcart and flatboat. Old photographs show that a balcony suspended over the main entrance originally extended to the columns.

In plan, a central hallway opens onto a back gallery on both floors. At some point in its evolution as a home, the house was expanded by adding, among other things, three bedrooms to the second floor. (Colonel Fort became the guardian of a niece and three nephews when his sister and her husband died of typhoid fever.) All new rooms

Ionic capital and porch entablature of the Fort House, Waco. (Photograph by J. Griffis Smith)

were contained within a double-galleried ell, which was laid out to maximize cross ventilation and onto which all but one of the bedrooms open. Other alterations included attaching the kitchen to the house, making a second parlor out of a room behind the first, and enlarging the dining room.

An 1873 bird's-eye map of Waco, drawn by one H. Brosius and discovered after the restoration, shows the Fort House after the wing was added sitting on almost an entire block, along with an assortment of "dependencies," or outbuildings, such as clapboard servants' quarters and a brick bathhouse.

Detail of a window head and cornice, Fort House, Waco. (Photograph by J. Griffis Smith)

The two downstairs parlors, separated by folding paneled doors, are said to have been the "center of much merriment and happy times" in the Fort household.[2] In them, supposedly, during the coming-out party for his daughter May and niece Catherine, the colonel served the first iced punch ever served in Waco. The parlors were also where May and Catherine entertained the young men who had followed family protocol by sending notes to the colonel at his office and to whom he had given his approval. The colonel gave his sons and nephews a good bit more latitude. One reason their upstairs bedrooms opened onto

the gallery was so that they could come and go without too many questions being asked.

After Dionitia Fort's death in 1910, the house passed from family ownership, changing title frequently and decaying rapidly until 1956, when it was bought by the Junior League. Then a group of interested citizens, led by Mrs. George Nalle and Lavonia Barnes, who were prime movers of the Earle-Harrison House restoration, bought the Fort House from the Junior League and commissioned Raiford to restore it.

Like the Earle-Harrison House, the Fort House had been pretty well messed up when it was divided into apartments. Nevertheless, all the original floors and ceilings downstairs were in good enough shape to restore, as was the main staircase and ban-

[2]"Fort House Museum," docent training material prepared by the Historic Waco Foundation (October, 1982), p. 4.

East Terrace, Waco. (Photograph by J. Griffis Smith)

ister. Raiford also removed all "tacked-on" structures—bathrooms and storage rooms that had been added to the house after the Fort family ceased to own it—and thoroughly cleaned the exterior, carefully sandblasting and waterproofing the brick, repointing joints and replacing brick where need be, and designing an exhibit space on the second floor.

Upon completion of the restoration in 1958, the house was presented to the citizens of Waco for community use. The Historic Waco Foundation now owns, maintains, and operates it, appropriately furnished, as a house museum. It too is listed on the National Register of Historic Places and is open to the public on weekends, from 2:00 to 5:00 P.M., and on other days by appointment.

Of the four houses that Raiford restored in Waco, perhaps the most historically significant is the one that is least like all the rest—East Terrace. Built around 1873 by Waco businessman John Wesley Mann (and sometimes called the Mann House), the house marked the arrival in Waco of a kind of transitional Victorian style that had been the rage back East for years. Whereas the Greek Revival was distinguished by its symmetry, center-hall plan, simple detailing, and clean, orderly lines, this so-called Italianate style expressed itself vertically in a flourish of off-center towers, tall windows and doors, thin columns, bay windows, and bracketed eaves.[3]

What makes East Terrace unique is that it was built almost a decade before the Italianate style became popular in Texas, which could have been due to the origins of Mrs. Mann. Cemira Twaddle Mann was born in 1847 and reared for twelve years in Poughkeepsie, New York, in a region where the style first took hold in the 1850s, and she may have influenced the design of her new Waco home by a nostalgic appreciation of her childhood surroundings. (An even earlier manifestation of the Italianate in Texas, Ashton Villa in Galveston, was built in 1859 and restored by Raiford in the early 1970s [see p. 134].)

Cemira's husband, John Wesley Mann, was a native of Tennessee who enlisted in the Confederate army as a private, serving as a scout until the war's end. Legend has it that he then walked all the way from Tennessee to Waco with his cousin, settling down and prospering over the years as the owner of a lumberyard, flour mill, and brick plant, among other businesses, and as a director of the First National Bank.

Due in part, perhaps, to its singularity in a Greek Revival town, the lavish home that John and Cemira built soon became one of Waco's most famous estates. The site was a fifteen-acre tract on the Brazos River that the Manns bought from T. H. Killingsworth

in 1873 for fifteen hundred dollars. Also called the "River House," the residence was built on the east bank of the Brazos and originally sat on a terrace of sand and clay reinforced by a brick wall (hence its more popular name), though by the time the house was restored in the early 1960s river silt had covered most of the terrace walls and the river itself had changed course so many times that it was some distance away. In its heyday, however, the East Terrace grounds, just a few feet from the river's edge, were full of strutting peacocks, deer, rose gardens, an orchard, a sunken garden with a goldfish pond, and terraces draped in columbine.

The house itself was built of the finest pink brick from the Mann kilns, which also supplied brick for Waco's famous suspension bridge over the Brazos (completed in 1870), as well as a number of houses and public buildings in town. It is said, in fact, that a standing order around the kilns was to stockpile all the best brick for Mr. Mann's future home. The quality of the brick is still quite evident in the semicircular window heads around the tops of the tall, arched windows, where each brick is keyed to form an almost perfect curve. Mann-made brick was also used in building the walkways, storm cellar, and the chimneys of the servants' quarters.

The front entrance to the house is beneath a two-story gallery with lathed balusters on the upper level. Double doors are framed by wide jambs on either side and topped with an arched pediment, which is supported by ornate, though well-proportioned, brackets. Original glass in the doors was etched camphor, depicting stags at a watering hole, but was replaced at some point by a reproduction after the original was broken.

The original part of the house, to which several additions were later made, contains an entrance hall and three rooms downstairs—Mann's office, sitting room, and parlor—and upstairs, a nursery, two bedrooms, and a smaller room from which a

[3]In architecture, the Victorian period (named for the queen of England whose reign it more or less paralleled [1837–1901]) was an amalgam of eclectic styles that would get even more extravagant as time wore on. After the Italianate would come High Victorian Gothic, Queen Anne, and Eastlake, all of which would fairly crackle with turrets, textures, pinnacles, patterns, dormers, gables, color, and ornament. The era also introduced a certain free-form functionalism to the layout of the house. Bursting out of the prescribed formality of the Greek Revival plan, Victorian rooms were arranged according to use and logical relationship. Dining rooms were placed close to kitchens, which were now attached to the house, and some of the finest houses began to feature indoor plumbing.

Front porch of East Terrace, Waco. (Photograph by J. Griffis Smith)

winding stairway leads up into the tower. (The tower, or cupola, served not only as a distinctive feature of the Italianate style but also as a "solar chimney," as energy-conscious architects call them today, ventilating hot air from the rest of the house.) The first kitchen was detached, standing on the east side of the house.

The first enlargement of the house, sometime in the early 1880s, was in the form of a two-story ell with double galleries and containing only one large room on each floor—the one downstairs serving as the dining room and the one upstairs as a kind of common bedroom that came to be called the "dormitory" (since it was often furnished with several beds). Attached to the house at some point, the kitchen was connected to the dining room by a large pantry, and over it was built a "cook's room" that was accessible only through the kitchen.

The last major addition was another two-story wing containing two parlors downstairs and a large ballroom upstairs, added to the house, as the docent literature points out, "with elegance and primarily for entertaining."[4] Part of this final addition was an upstairs bathroom, complete with a cast-iron bathtub trimmed in walnut and decorated with cavorting water nymphs.

After Mann's death in 1919, East Terrace was never quite the same. Cemira continued to live there until the late twenties,

[4] "East Terrace," docent training material prepared by the Historic Waco Foundation, n.d., p. 4.

Brackets and arched pediment above the front door of East Terrace, Waco. (Photograph by J. Griffis Smith)

when she went to live with a son. Shortly thereafter the house was leased by Dr. and Mrs. C. C. Lemly and operated for five years as a nursing home. Finally, in 1960, the Young Brothers construction company gave the house and a small part of the grounds to the Heritage Society of Waco, which commissioned Raiford to restore it. As in his other brick-house restorations in Waco, most of the work involved repairing, replacing, and waterproofing the brick, which—though more "perfect" than brick on the other jobs—was made from the same soft, sandy clay and hadn't endured the elements any better. For repointing the joints, Raiford also worked out a formula to match

the color of the original mortar, playing with certain ratios of white cement, gray cement, and lime until he got it just right. Refurnished as the fine Victorian home that it was for some fifty years and listed on the National Register, East Terrace is owned, maintained, and operated by the Historic Waco Foundation as a house museum, open to the public on weekends from 2:00 to 5:00 P.M. and on other days by appointment. The house and its remaining grounds may also be rented for special occasions, and though the grounds are not as large or lavish as they were in the late 1800s, East Terrace is one of the most popular "party houses" in town.

Milton Garrett House, San Augustine. (Photograph by J. Griffis Smith)

Restoration of the Milton Garrett House, Stephen W. Blount House, Matthew
Cartwright House, and Ezekiel Cullen House, San Augustine

After his divorce in 1947, Raiford's return to San Augustine was less than triumphant, but it turned out to be one of the best things ever to happen to him and to his hometown. Even if progress bypasses a community, leaving its old architecture intact, buildings will suffer from neglect and misuse, which can be worse than new construction. When Raiford came home to stay, San Augustine gained a feisty, homegrown architect who had developed a certain expertise in historic preservation and who would like nothing better than to spend the rest of his career saving the oldest houses in the county.

The oldest house Raiford has managed to save so far in or around San Augustine is indeed the oldest in the county and was for several years his own home—the Milton Garrett House (see chapter 1), a log house built in 1826 about ten miles west of town on the old Camino Real. Milton Garrett was the second son of Jacob Garrett, an early settler of the area and prominent early Texan who received from the Mexican government a land grant that would become one of San Augustine County's largest plantations. While Jacob's oldest son William would eventually build a big plantation house east toward town, Milton would be satisfied with a small (18-by-30-foot) log house he built near a spring where Indians used to camp and from which his descendants would draw water well into the twentieth century.

It was built as a single-pen, story-and-a-half house with square logs, dovetail joints, detached kitchen, open porches front and back, and a fireplace and chimney on each end made by slaves out of blue-marl stone, a local rock that has a blue tint when first cut but turns buff pink as the iron in it oxidizes. Downstairs, the house was divided into two rooms, with front doors opening into both. A steep stair in the front corner by the fireplace on the west end leads up to "the boys' room." Mantels on both fireplaces are superbly crafted, Raiford says, probably copied from a classical design in a builder's handbook and enhanced in the west-end bedroom by an equally well-crafted jack arch that forms the top of the fireplace opening.

Originally designed as a vernacular log house, and precisely as Raiford has restored it, the Garrett House features little ornament to speak of, save for a nail pattern on one door—and a bullet hole. And therein lies a tale. According to Raiford, one of Buddy Garrett's favorite stories was one about two horse thieves who spent the night upstairs in the boys' room, having stopped and asked for a night's lodging without, of course, revealing their true intent. The next morning, one of the men came down the stairs gripping a horse pistol, and when he got about halfway down he fired a shot just to frighten everyone off. The bullet went through the front door of the west room, which was open, pierced the partition, and traveled out a bedroom window. "Old man Garrett had gotten suspicious and had had the niggers hide the horses the day before," Raiford says. "They didn't get any horses but they did scare old lady Garrett, who was cooking breakfast on the fireplace."

Raiford has been interested in the Garrett House since the 1920s, when he took a se-

Dovetail joints on the Milton Garrett House, San Augustine. (Photograph by J. Griffis Smith)

ries of photographs of it, but it wasn't until the late 1960s that he was finally able to talk the last Garrett owner and occupant, also named Milton, into selling it. "I came by here one day," Raiford says, "and some of the family had put a chain link fence out there. And I said, 'Milton, if you ever do sell me this durn old place, I'll give you that fence and you can put it around that family cemetery back there.' I wanted to put back the old split-rail fence that was there when I took a picture of it in 1927. And that turned the deal."

When Raiford bought the house in 1970 (paying Milton Garrett cash), it had never had a coat of paint. Logs had been covered with lapped siding—probably right before the Civil War, Raiford theorizes—and a wing on each end of the house had been added at some point and taken away at another (investigating the site, Raiford found the remnants of fireplace foundations at an appropriate distance from each end). The back porch had also been enclosed and made into a kitchen and bedroom.

While keeping the porch enclosed and turning the bedroom into a bathroom and closet, Raiford set out to "put it back like it was." He took the siding off the two end walls to expose the logs (he has since replaced it on the east wall to protect some rotting timber); repointed the blue-marl chimneys; rechinked the exposed logs with a modern-day mixture of mud, Spanish moss, sand, and mason's cement; replaced all the floors except the one in the east room, which is original virgin pine; replaced two pole rafters in the roof (all the rest are original); replaced the chamfered posts on the front porch; and coated all wood surfaces with a colorless preservative that he also used on Independence Hall (see p. 138).

Notwithstanding a somewhat lifeless blue-gray pallor the preservative gives to the wood, the Milton Garrett House is "put back like it was" with an artful understanding of history and a sensitive feel for what makes a good home. (The project was, after all, one of the closest things Raiford has done to an "adaptive reuse," though the house was not adapted for any kind of different purpose.) For years Raiford maintained it as a weekend house, then lived comfortably in it for about three years, until his eyes went bad and until the logging truck hit him as he was turning into the driveway. Now he keeps it as a kind of guest house and as a featured attraction on the annual "Medallion Homes and Historical

Places" tour sponsored by the Ezekiel Cullen Chapter of the DRT.

Of the ten historic structures that Raiford has restored in San Augustine, his favorites are three Greek Revival houses that are all that remain here of the designs of Augustus Phelps. Little is known of this Vermont tradesman who migrated to San Augustine by way of Philadelphia in 1838, for he didn't stay here long, moving on to Austin where he died in 1841 at the age of twenty-eight while working on plans for a new capitol. But the brevity of his stay in San Augustine (and on earth) was more than made up for by the quality of his work. In addition to a builder's handbook, Phelps possessed a sharp eye for detail and proportion and a steady hand for execution that would have been the envy of any self-styled "architect" of the 1830s.

His first contract upon arrival in San Augustine was to build a house for Col. Stephen William Blount, who had been elected as a delegate to the convention at Washington-on-the-Brazos not long after settling here in 1835 and was one of the signers of the Texas Declaration of Independence in March of 1836. Establishing himself in the mercantile business in San Augustine, Blount would also be elected county clerk when the county was organized in 1846 and serve for a time as postmaster.

It has been written that the Blount House "exemplifies the spirit of the man," in reference to Colonel Blount, who was known for his energy and generosity.[5] But as far as Raiford is concerned, the man whose spirit this house exemplifies is Phelps, who "had to sell himself" with his first job, as Raiford says, trying his best to impress the town with his New England craftsmanship and knowledge of the Greek Revival, which was still gaining in popularity back East. Arriv-

[5] Anne Clark, *Historic Homes of San Augustine* (Austin: Encino Press, 1972), p. 24.

Stephen W. Blount House, San Augustine. (Photograph by J. Griffis Smith)

ing in San Augustine when he did, Phelps was also able to take advantage of one of the earliest sawmills in the county, which began operating in the early 1800s (see footnote 5, chapter 1) and did much to facilitate the San Augustine boom.

Applying classic Greek details to a one-story, 37-by-18-foot wood-frame house, Phelps formed the front portico with a pediment, Doric entablature, and two fluted Doric columns, connecting the columns to the house by a diamond lattice-work. All trim is double beaded with medallion corners on door and window surrounds, and pilasters define the corners of the original house, the entablature of which features a frieze of "triglyphs" and "metopes," characteristic ornament of the Doric order that can be found on the Parthenon itself. (Triglyphs consist of raised blocks of three vertical bands that alternate with metopes, which can be plain or sculp-

tured panels. Above the triglyphs are "mutules," blocks with three rows of six square pegs, or "guttae," fastened to the sloping soffit. At the bottom of each triglyph is a single row of six guttae.)

About the only concession Phelps made to classical Rome is the arched doorway with an inverted five-pointed star carved in the keystone. Phelps's affinity for the Texas star (which would also be a recurring motif in the regional architecture of David Williams a century later) also shows up in the pressed-metal leader heads, each stamped with the year "1839" as well as nine stars right side up, on all four corners of the original house. Poured glass for the windows came from Birmingham, Alabama, through New Orleans, then up the Red River and overland to San Augustine. (Some of this glass still exists in all three of the surviving Phelps houses in San Augustine.)

Pedimented portico on the Stephen W. Blount House, San Augustine. (Photograph by J. Griffis Smith)

All this intricate detailing absolutely bowls Raiford over. In all his years of restoration work, in San Augustine and elsewhere, he's never seen anything quite like it. He's convinced that it makes the Blount House one of the best examples of Greek Revival architecture in the country, even though its one-story height—made to seem even lower by later additions—makes it less grand an example than, say, the Earle-Harrison House in Waco.

Part of what impresses Raiford so much about the detailing of the Blount House, he says, is the fact that it was all done by hand.

Although the new sawmill supplied the lumber, the triglyphs and guttae had to be cut by hand and fastened to the frieze and soffit by square nails, which didn't exactly allow the most finesse. Since the square nail was sharp only on its four edges (the end was blunt), it pushed a plug of wood ahead of itself, which made it impossible for the nail to slide between the grains of wood. Hence, the smaller the piece of wood the more likely it was to split, and, as Raiford points out, "They didn't have any glue to stick it." Raiford also marvels at the precision workmanship evident in the columns,

Latticework on the portico of the Stephen W. Blount House, San Augustine. (Photograph by Mark Meyer)

each of which shows the proper entasis (the convex curve of the shaft), no mean feat when the columns had to be cut and put together with square nails out of two-flute strips. Raiford says that capitals for the columns were turned by a mule-powered lathe.

As the Blount family grew, two wings were added, first on the east side, then on the west, making for a kind of sprawling effect on the form of the house that seems to dilute its Greek Revival flavor (although this central block flanked by lower wings is a kind of Palladian form much admired by Thomas Jefferson, who used one-story projections on each side to break out of the two-story Georgian box). At one point, an office that Colonel Blount attached to the end of the west wing raised the ire of a neighbor who insisted that it stuck too far out into the street, so the colonel moved it around and attached it to the back of the wing. Other additions were made at the back of the house, including two shed rooms with ceilings considerably lower than the original twelve-foot, four-inch ceilings in the central block.

Inside the original part of the house, the

Leader head on the Stephen W. Blount House, San Augustine. (Photograph by Mark Meyer)

Arch with inverted five-pointed star above the doorway, Stephen W. Blount House, San Augustine. (Photograph by Mark Meyer)

high ceilings make the two front rooms seem as deep as wells, an effect accentuated by their fairly short lengths and widths. (As a New Englander, Raiford says, Phelps was "more or less dedicated to small rooms.") Walls in the major rooms were originally wainscoted and, above that, plastered over a stick lath. The walls of Blount's controversial office were papered directly onto wood.

Raiford bought the Blount House himself in the early fifties to restore, inhabit, and work in (see chapter 1), his first "adaptive reuse" (though like the Garrett House almost twenty years later, he would restore it to use as it was originally intended). In the process he came to admire Phelps for his skill and technique even more. Raiford discovered an original half-round gutter in the attic of the main part of the house, covered by the shed roof of one of the additions, which was made from a single log, thirty-six feet long, lined with metal and faced with hand-planed Greek molding. Raiford

also found that the plaster for the walls was made of lime putty, sand, and cow hair, which served as a binder.

Raiford's restoration of the house, which has been more or less ongoing for the last thirty years, has involved repairing and repainting the exterior pine siding and detailing, scraping down and refinishing the pine floors and woodwork, and reinforcing the foundation and frame where necessary. The only addition that was removed was a dining room added to the back when the Blount House served as a boardinghouse years ago. Raiford has also managed to duplicate the striped wallpaper Colonel Blount put on his office walls.

Even while Raiford owned it, the Blount House served a wide variety of purposes— home, office, "YMCA," historically significant work of Republic of Texas architecture. Still a San Augustine landmark, the house is now owned by Raiford's son Raggy, who lives in it with his wife and two daughters.

Matthew Cartwright House, San Augustine. (Photograph by J. Griffis Smith)

The second house Phelps designed and built in San Augustine was the Matthew Cartwright House, the only one of Raiford's three Phelps restorations that is a full two stories in height and the only one without a predominant, pedimented porch. At first glance, in fact, this modest portico seems almost like a tacked-on addition to a Georgian- or Federal-style house that the owner simply wanted to update. Upon closer inspection, however, the house represents the Greek Revival at its most elegant.

The most common conception of the Greek Revival house is that of a two-story mansion with enormous, full-width porch. And if the Parthenon were used as a model, then the house would have to be front

gabled as well, its roof ridge perpendicular to the street. The fact is that the style was incorporated in bits and pieces, and as simple Texas farmhouses were customized with Greek Revival details, residences in town were often designed with a certain sophisticated restraint, particularly if the style had just arrived. Although the Cartwright House is indeed side gabled and features a rather puny porch, the heavy pediments on the ends of its gabled roof and the bold entablature of the porch and house proper, along with two fluted Doric columns on the porch, indicate that it is very much a Greek Revival structure.

Phelps actually built the house in 1839 for the brother-in-law of Cartwright's wife, Isaac

Front porch with bold entablature and Doric columns on the Matthew Cartwright House, San Augustine. (Photograph by Mark Meyer)

Campbell, who was appointed to a committee to select a site for the capital of the Republic of Texas and moved from San Augustine not long after the house was built. It then served as college classroom space, situated as it was across the street from San Augustine University. In 1847, the house was bought by Cartwright, who had come to the San Augustine area from Tennessee with his parents when he was fourteen. He would later fight in the Texas Revolution at the siege of Bexar and the battle of Concepción, and during a minor prelude to the battle of San Jacinto, his horse was shot out from under him. Cartwright went on to amass a fortune in real estate, acquiring more than a million acres by trading for sections awarded to veterans of the Texas Revolution at a time when land was cheap and unsettled and when few people realized what it was going to be worth. He would also operate a profitable mercantile business that his father began on the courthouse square in the 1830s.

One of the most interesting aspects of his house, Raiford says, is the assortment of detached structures still scattered around it. Contained within the original picket fence

Dependency on the grounds of the Matthew Cartwright House, San Augustine. (Photograph by Mark Meyer)

are a toolhouse, servants' quarters, privy, well house, and carriage house—some of which are as well built and detailed as the house itself. (There is also a detached office on the grounds.) In addition, there is a one-story ell attached to the back and two huge fireplaces at either end of the main structure, one of which features a mantel marble-ized by Phelps himself, who excelled in that decorative technique as much as he did in carpentry and design. Although Phelps was indeed a master of many crafts, it is said that during the construction of the Cartwright House, the narrow "New England" stair that he specified was so difficult to build that another San Augustine master builder, Gen. T. G. Broocks, was brought in for that purpose.

Kept in the Cartwright family since Matthew bought it in 1847, the house has been well lived in over the years. Raiford's restoration, done in phases during the 1950s, mainly involved refurbishing what had always been pretty well maintained—repainting, repointing, and repairing where need be and generally making sure that whatever was done to the house was in keeping with its original design (though Raiford chose not to replace the double-hung Victorian windows that had been in-stalled on the first floor, which differ from the original windows by having four lights, or panes, in each sash rather than six). The house is now listed on the National Register of Historic Places and is owned and oc-cupied by Mrs. Mintie Cartwright Kardell.

Ezekiel Cullen House, San Augustine. (Photograph by J. Griffis Smith)

The Greek Revival features of the third Phelps-built residence in San Augustine, the Ezekiel Cullen House, are more pronounced than those of the Cartwright House. Taking up almost its entire front, the pediment, entablature, and columns are of the classic Greek-temple form—massive gabled end of the roof turned to the street, pulled out to extend over the porch, and supported by four widely spaced Doric columns (this "tetrastyle" portico is so big, in fact, that it seems to belong on a two-story house). An operable fanlight in the center of the pediment (repeated on the back of the house) not only adds a decorative touch but also lights and ventilates the "attic," which is actually a full-length garret where dances were often held.

Although the detail is more subdued on the Cullen House than on the Blount House (there are no triglyphs or metopes on the frieze of the entablature), there are a number of similarities, including the columns, latticework, and leader heads—which may have served no function at all since they are positioned so the downspout would have run down the corner columns. There are also corner medallions on the door and window frames, as well as a five-pointed star above the double-front door, though this one is larger and right side up.

The star is larger, Raiford theorizes, because of the local eminence of Ezekiel Cullen, for whom Phelps built the house in 1839. Cullen came to Texas from Georgia with a law degree in 1835, setting up practice in San Augustine and going on to serve as a district judge and state representative.

Fanlight in the center of the pediment on the Ezekiel Cullen House, San Augustine. (Photograph by Mark Meyer)

As a member of the Third Texas Congress in 1839, he sponsored a bill that eventually set aside 221,420 acres of public land for the "establishment and endowment of two colleges or Universities," which would result in the Permanent University Fund and the UT-A&M building boom on which Raiford cut his teeth as an architect.

After the Civil War, the house became the property of Benjamin Roberts, whose father, Elisha, was one of San Augustine's founding fathers. (It is said that in 1822, Elisha was hot on the trail of a runaway slave when he passed through what is now San Augustine. So impressed was he by the

surrounding countryside that he vowed to return here with his family and put down roots.) Finally, in 1952, Judge Cullen's grandson, wealthy Houston wildcatter Hugh Roy Cullen, bought the house back and commissioned Raiford to restore it for presentation to the Ezekiel Cullen Chapter of the DRT.

It was one of Raiford's first restoration jobs after the war, and, like La Bahía in the sixties, a project in which money was practically no object. Raiford started by removing all the tacked-on structures that were part of a remodeling in the early 1900s, leaving twelve feet that Judge Cullen had added

Leader head minus downspout on the Ezekiel Cullen House, San Augustine. (Photograph by Mark Meyer)

to the side of the house. Raiford also left a stair inside that had replaced the original, and characteristically steep, Phelps-built stair. Upstairs in the garret, Raiford cleared out partitions that had gone in over the years to divide it into bedrooms and returned the space to its glory as one big ballroom.

Given to the DRT in 1953 and furnished with period pieces—including a mahogany wardrobe in which Sam Houston once stored his uniforms—the Cullen House is now the headquarters of San Augustine's Ezekiel Cullen Chapter. It is also listed on the National Register of Historic Places and is open to the public on alternate Sundays during the spring and summer and on other days by appointment.

The French Legation, Austin. (Photograph by J. Griffis Smith)

Restoration of the French Legation, Austin

The Colorado River spills out of the Texas Hill Country through valleys and canyons of limestone outcroppings. But before it cuts into the flatter coastal plain to the south, the river meanders past a few gentle rises. It was this section of the river valley that caught the attention of Mirabeau Buonaparte Lamar in 1839 as he searched for a new capital site for the Republic of Texas.

In the same year, a young French diplomat named Jean Pierre Isidore Alphonse Dubois traveled to Texas on assignment to assess the new nation. Dubois—later assuming the suffix "de Saligny" and not bothering to correct anyone who addressed him as "Count"—visited Galveston, Hous-

ton, and Matagorda, and his favorable reports influenced France's recognition of the independent Republic of Texas.

Dubois returned to Texas in 1840 and presented credentials declaring himself the French chargé d'affaires. Traveling to the new capital on the Colorado River at Austin—named for the Republic's venerable patron of organized Anglo settlement, Stephen Fuller Austin—Dubois soon raised the ire of his new neighbors. In the midst of passing bogus money, instructing a servant to slaughter someone else's hogs, and generally forfeiting neutrality in stormy Texas politics, Dubois managed to buy a fine piece of property east of the new capitol site. On one of those graceful rises over-

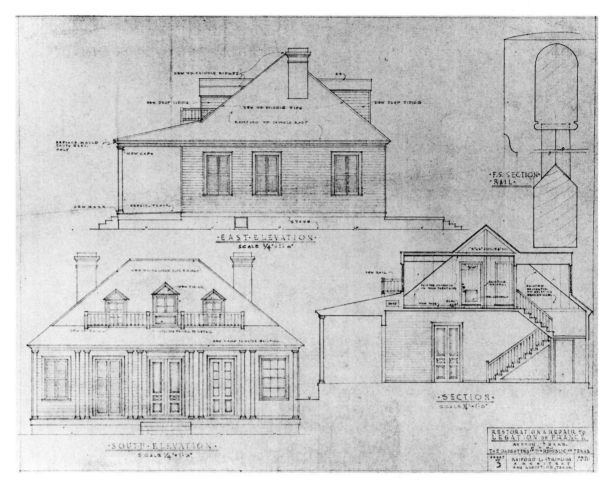

Raiford's drawings of the elevations of the French Legation, Austin.

looking the river, he began the construction of his home and office, styled as a legation of the French government.

Influenced by the architecture developed in French colonies of the Caribbean and transplanted to Louisiana, the small frame house was built of native pine from Bastrop and exhibits a number of distinctive French features. Beneath a sweeping hipped roof, French doors open onto a finely proportioned Louisiana porch supported by paired columns and facing south toward the river. Dormer windows illuminate attic space above (originally used as servants' quarters), and a wine cellar is dug into the sturdy hilltop

below a central hallway. (Raiford says the Violet Crown Garden Club of Austin, when it was custodian of the site, installed a sprinkler system that flooded the wine cellar every time it was turned on, which forced him to install a sump pump in the cellar so he could routinely bail it out whenever the lawn was watered.) Dubois is said to have brought hardware for doors and windows from London, although no record of where he purchased his furnishings has been found.

The framework of the house is also somewhat distinctive, indicating the work of an experienced craftsman. The foundation

Restored stable at the French Legation, Austin, now the museum shop and office for the Daughters of the Republic of Texas. (Photograph by J. Griffis Smith)

frame is made of oak and juniper timbers, which probably came from the original twenty-one-acre site, hand-adzed and hand-squared and connected with chiseled joints and wooden pegs. Rafters are fastened together with large square nails.

Soon after the diplomat moved into his house, he arranged for its sale to a close friend and confidant, the Reverend John Mary Odin, later the bishop of the Roman Catholic diocese of Texas. The agreement called for Dubois to finish the house and to build a kitchen and stable before he moved; he evidently did so in haste. Failure of the Texas Congress to pass the Franco-Texian Bill, which would have allowed armed French colonization in Texas in return for a

sizable loan, left Dubois little for which to lobby. He withdrew to Louisiana in 1841 and never returned to Austin.

In 1847 Albert Sidney Burleson negotiated with Bishop Odin's agent for the purchase of the Dubois house, while Odin in the meantime sold it to Moseley Baker. Before Baker could rightfully claim ownership, however, Burleson helped himself to several pieces of furniture belonging to Dubois. This mix-up probably preserved the furnishings, many of which were later returned to the house after recognition of its historical significance. In 1848 Moseley sold the house to Dr. Joseph W. Robertson, whose family would make some modifications and additions over the years (parti-

Restored privy at the French Legation, Austin. (Photograph by J. Griffis Smith)

tioning the attic into a bedroom and bath, among other things), but the Robertsons can also be credited with maintaining it practically intact until 1948, when they sold it for about forty thousand dollars to the state of Texas, which assigned custodianship of the property to the DRT.

The DRT asked Raiford in 1955 to investigate the site and restore the structure to its appearance during the time Dubois represented the French government in Texas. Displeased with a rock fence that the Violet Crown Garden Club put up in the 1930s (among other alterations of the landscape), Raiford called in a University of Texas team of archaeologists to set the grounds record straight. His own investigation of the house revealed that Dubois, in his hasty completion of it, had stretched painted canvas between bare studs to finish out the walls inside. The canvas itself was eventually covered with wallboard. Among other things, Raiford also removed the bedroom and bathroom from the attic, repaired rotted

Chimney of the French Legation, Austin. (Photograph by J. Griffis Smith)

portions of the porch, and replaced deteriorated timbers and boards throughout the house.

Archaeologists located the sites of the former kitchen and privy, and in 1967 the DRT contracted Raiford to reconstruct these two dependencies. Basing his designs on Dubois's records, archaeological findings, and the memories of Robertson family members, Raiford produced two frame structures to complement the Legation and its peaceful hilltop. (HABS drawings in the Library of Congress posed a problem early on, showing the detached kitchen to have been at the northwest corner of the house, which contradicted the archaeology. After learning from one of the Robertsons that the kitchen had actually been at the north-

east corner, Raiford and the archaeologists determined that the northwest corner had been the site of the privy.) In 1974 he once again drew plans for the last-known 1840s structure recorded on the site—a one-and-a-half-story, wood-frame stable adapted for use as the DRT office and museum shop.

Owned by the state of Texas and maintained and operated by the DRT as a house museum, the French Legation is open to the public from 1:00 to 5:00 P.M. Tuesday through Sunday, free of charge. DRT docents guide tours through the main house, including the attic and wine cellar, and through the completely stocked detached kitchen. The Legation is also listed on the National Register of Historic Places.

Restoring Texas

Ashton Villa, Galveston. (Photograph by J. Griffis Smith)

Restoration of Ashton Villa, Galveston

The natural harbor nestled behind Galveston Island attracted European explorers for years before it became a major Republic of Texas port. French surveyors around 1780 named the harbor for Bernardo de Gálvez, governor of Louisiana; a later Frenchman who knew a safe harbor when he saw one—pirate Jean Laffite—established the first European settlement on the island in 1817. Then, with Texas independence secured in 1836, the port city boomed. Its heady atmosphere attracted trade, bold business ventures, and adventurous young men, whose badly needed skills could be quickly built into fortunes and prestige in the young Republic.

John Moreau Brown was one of the thousands of United States citizens whose pursuit of opportunity led to Texas. Born to Dutch parents in New York State in 1821, Brown worked as a brickmason's apprentice before setting out along the trade routes of the Ohio and Mississippi rivers. Raiford likes to point out that Brown's business was

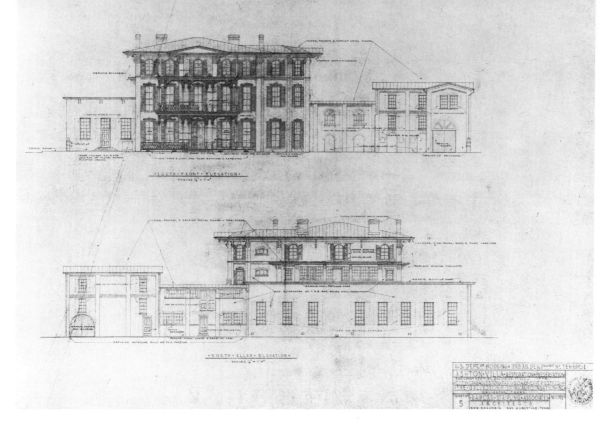

Raiford's drawings of the elevations for Ashton Villa, Galveston.

to build brick cisterns, and the Easterner got to Galveston by building "cisterns from Pennsylvania south."

Brown obviously had a good background in structures, Raiford adds, as evidenced by the house he built here in 1859. Brown had married Rebecca Ashton Stoddart in 1847, and within a decade had amassed enough wealth, and children, to justify a palatial home in his adopted city. With strong connections to the East—Rebecca was from Philadelphia—Brown named the house Ashton Villa, after her family, and chose the Italianate style for its design, which was then fashionable on the East Coast. It is also the same style that John Wesley Mann would adopt for his East Terrace in Waco in 1873 (see p. 112), but since Galveston was a port of entry for fashion as well as goods and people, new styles would appear here first, then trickle inland.

According to Raiford, however, the symmetry of Ashton Villa's front bay, and its graceful detailing inside, reflect the interest in the Greek Revival style that was still quite popular in Galveston in the late 1850s. Even though the house appeared at first glance to be a radical departure from the norm, its symmetry and detailing probably put the neighbors at ease, if not in awe.

Evidently producing the bricks in his own kilns, Brown imported other fixtures to accent the Italianate design. Although Galveston industry might have been capable of producing cast-iron lintels, balconies, and fences, Raiford is convinced these items were shipped from Philadelphia. Brown is said to have imported plantings from Europe, and even two hundred English sparrows to protect the valuable flora from local insects. Raiford points to the sitting room's pocket sliding doors and notes that they are exactly as detailed in one of the most popular builder's handbooks of the day, Lefever's 1835 *The Beauties of Modern Architecture*.

During the Civil War, Brown and his family fled to the mainland as Union ships shelled the island and eventually obtained its surrender in June of 1865. Some surrender ceremonies are said to have taken place in Ashton Villa, and both Confederate and Union officials might have used it for headquarters, since it was shielded from the shelling and remained one of the premier structures on the island. (After the war, the island as a whole was shielded from the effects of a destroyed economy, thriving as a major financial and cotton-processing center as well as shipping point in the late nineteenth century.)

A large vaulted family room and a conservatory were added to the rear of the house before 1865. Ashton Villa's east dining room and the corresponding upstairs bedrooms were extended in the late 1890s. The result was an overall asymmetry not unsuited to the original exterior styling, as broad-bracketed eaves, brick, and cast-iron detailing were extended around this new east wing. Brown's building expertise was confirmed when the infamous 1900 hurricane swept over the island, easily destroying lesser structures. Ashton Villa's only loss was three feet of its foundation when a subsequent grade-raising project sought to minimize the flooding damage of future hurricanes. Because earth fill was brought in, neither the house nor the cast-iron fence was moved.

Brown's daughter, "Miss Bettie" as Raiford calls her, died in 1920, and the house sat neglected until acquired by the Galveston Shriners in 1927. As the El Mina Shrine Temple, the house was spared major structural or decorative changes, though the Shriners did remove the rear dependencies and attach a large, but sympathetic, brick wing extending from the northeast. In 1971 the Shriners sold Ashton Villa to the city of Galveston for $125,000, and a drive was launched to restore the elegance of the house to the era of the Brown family's ownership and occupation.

Raiford began the restoration in 1973, praising the fine craftsmanship and referring to Ashton Villa as "one of the most

Window detail, Ashton Villa, Galveston. (Photograph by J. Griffis Smith)

outstanding residences that has been constructed in the South." The thirteen-inch-thick brick walls made the job easier, he says, because they prevented condensation, or 'sweating,' on the inside plaster walls. The job was also made easier by the amount of documentation available showing the house as it was in the 1800s. "I had more photographic information to work from on this house than any restoration I've ever done," Raiford says. Window arrangements changed by the Shriners in the late 1920s were returned to their original configurations, tongue-in-groove flooring was lovingly repaired, and missing tiles around the fireplaces were painstakingly matched and replaced. Conditions of a federal grant for restoring the house caused a few headaches, Raiford remembers, explaining how

Cast-iron detailing, Ashton Villa, Galveston. (Photograph by J. Griffis Smith)

return-air ducts had to be custom formed and fitted between the walls.

The project also involved replacing the porch's octagonal quarry tile, which is no longer manufactured and had to be duplicated by carefully cutting modern-day tile; reproducing original column capitals on the porch deck and missing brackets on the cornice; repairing or replacing shutters; raising the cast-iron entry steps; repairing the standing-seam tin roof; and turning around thousands of bricks in the exterior walls, which had deteriorated or been painted over the years, so that the bricks would blend as well as they did originally.

According to Ashton Villa director Judy Schiebel, this impressively designed, built, and restored home may have exerted some influence on preeminent New York architect Philip Johnson, who called her to find out

what the original color of the mansion's cast-iron detailing was. According to Raiford it was white, information that Johnson wanted for the design of a mixed-use complex under construction in Dallas called The Crescent, scheduled to be completed in 1986 and whose design is derived from "Texas old-world architecture."[6]

Ashton Villa, a National Register landmark, is owned by the city of Galveston and leased for ten dollars a year to the Galveston Historical Foundation, which maintains and operates it as a house museum, open to the public from 10:00 A.M. to 4:00 P.M. on weekdays and 11:30 A.M. to 4:00 P.M. on weekends.

[6]"In Progress," *Texas Architect* (January-February, 1984): 93.

Independence Hall at Washington-on-the-Brazos. (Photograph by J. Griffis Smith)

Reconstruction of Independence Hall, Washington-on-the-Brazos

It is one thing to restore a historic building that has been fairly well cared for over the years, and it is quite another to rebuild one from scratch. The degree of certainty about a building's past is directly proportional to the amount of the building that still stands. The more that exists, the more that is known and the more than can be surmised. And if there is nothing to begin with, final interpretations are almost always the subject of debate.

Raiford nevertheless has found a good deal of excitement in the detective work required in reconstruction, relying on the professional findings of others as well as his own instincts. And no reconstruction has given him more satisfaction than Independence Hall at Washington-on-the-Brazos,

where the Texas Declaration of Independence was signed in March of 1836 (see p. 94).

He is particularly proud of the project because of its historical significance. Forty-four delegates gathered here on March 1, when the town was simply called Washington, a bustling new settlement near the La Bahía Road and the junction of the Brazos and Navasota rivers. The object of their gathering was to hammer out a document declaring Texas an autonomous nation, just as the thirteen American colonies had done for themselves sixty years before. The setting was considerably less stately than Independence Hall in Philadelphia, however, and considerably cooler than Philadelphia in July. Delegates met in an unfinished frame building that had just been rented by a group of civic leaders who were competing for the convention with a more established town down the Brazos. And according to the diary of William Fairfax Gray, a blue norther had blown in the night before, and "[i]n lieu of glass, cotton cloth was stretched across the windows, which partially excluded the cold wind."[7]

Had Texas remained a republic, perhaps its humble birthplace would have been enshrined. As it was, Texas eventually became a state, and the building in which independence from Mexico was declared went on to serve a number of more pedestrian purposes—church, dance hall, courthouse, dry-goods store, residence—finally burning down sometime between 1861 and 1899, when an obelisk was placed to mark the spot. In 1915 a state park was established to commemorate the declaration signing, and in 1926 a small white frame building was constructed near the existing markers as a replica of the hall, based on a photograph of the building taken sometime in the 1880s or 1890s.

Although Raiford's reconstruction of Independence Hall was thoroughly researched, the findings were far from conclusive. "For some unaccountable reason," wrote project historian R. Henderson Shuffler in 1962 for the *Southwestern Historical Quarterly*, "the building in which the convention of 1836 met has been one of the least-known structures in Texas history. There is an amazing confusion of opinion concerning its size, shape, and exact location and an equally amazing lack of documentary evidence concerning these matters."[8] (Since moved out of the park, the first facsimile, as Raiford says, "ain't Independence Hall a-tall.")

Raiford began the reconstruction in the summer of 1969. He had been commissioned by the state to build a structure that looked exactly like the one in which the declaration was signed, but there wasn't a whole lot to go on. The old photograph of "Independence Hall" was impossible to authenticate; even if it was genuine, it indicated that the building had been remodeled after 1836 since it didn't jibe with descriptions given by men who attended the convention and later reported on it. Gray wrote in his diary of "an unfinished house, without doors or windows." W. P. Zuber wrote years later that the building "was a two-story frame," twenty by forty feet, with two doors and an exterior stair. Dr. John Washington Lockhart described the hall as a "one-story house with the gable toward the street," "a double door in the center of the end opening on the street," and five or six windows. As for orientation, Zuber said the building faced north; Lockhart said west; and Frank Brown, who saw the building in 1861, remembered it facing Main Street.[9]

Archaeological investigations during the summer of 1964 revealed the remnants of postholes, trash pits, and a fireplace, verifying the location of a building—precisely where the 1899 marker said Independence Hall had been—and indicating the likely dimensions of a structure that roughly fit a kind of composite description. There was enough agreement on materials and size, as Shuffler writes, to come up with "a few reasonable deductions." It was safe to assume that the hall was a simple frame structure, probably a high-gabled story and a half and anywhere from twenty to twenty-five feet in width by thirty-five to fifty feet in length. Chances are it was also newly built of handhewn white oak and post oak on a cedar-block foundation, with clapboard siding and hand-split shingles.

Basing his design on those deductions, and on what his own nose for nineteenth-century construction could tell him, Raiford rebuilt the structure out of the varieties of oak used in the original, importing the

[7]R. Henderson Shuffler, "The Signing of Texas' Declaration of Independence: Myth and Record," *Southwestern Historical Quarterly* 65 (July, 1961–April, 1962); 327.
[8]Ibid., p. 312.
[9]Ibid., pp. 316–17.

white oak he needed from Tennessee. Assuming that the siding and shingles remained more or less constant during the various remodelings, Raiford referred to the photograph to determine the appropriate number of boards for the side of the building and shingles for the roof. To give the siding a rough finish, boards were cut 2 inches thick and 6¾ inches wide, then hand planed. Raiford made the siding thick enough to insulate the interior yet appear to be the standard half inch in thickness by cutting a U-shaped groove on the top and bottom of each board so that, when viewing the wall from the inside as well as out, the edges of the boards seem to overlap.

Raiford was concerned about insulation because of the comfort factor. Although made to look every bit as unfinished as the original, complete with unceiled roof and walls, Independence Hall is a good bit more cozy for the benefit of today's tourists than it was for the delegates to the convention in 1836. One of Raiford's biggest challenges was to figure out a way to conceal the air-conditioning system, which he did by running the ductwork from beneath the floor and hiding it under the display cases, along with the electric lighting. (Parks and Wildlife has since removed the display cases to make the hall more authentic, although grills for the ducts are now visible in the hardwood floor and artificial lighting is provided by electric lights along the walls that look like candles.)

Another concern, Raiford says, was how to make the building easy for Parks and Wildlife to maintain. He achieved that, in part, by sandwiching a metal roof between two layers of shingles and roof insulation, so that the roof looks like the same roof inside and out and won't require a lot of care to keep from leaking. He also put shutters on the windows and coated the siding with the same preservative he later used on the Garrett House in San Augustine (see p. 118).

Although somewhat overshadowed by the nearby Star of the Republic Museum, Independence Hall is operated by the Parks and Wildlife Department as the rightful centerpiece of the Washington-on-the-Brazos State Historical Park and is open to the public from 10:00 A.M. to 5:00 P.M., seven days a week.

Design of Sabine County Hospital, Hemphill

The residents of Sabine County—which borders San Augustine County to the east—had never really had a full-fledged hospital. In the 1920s, a six-bed clinic was built above a drugstore in Hemphill, the county seat, but after its proprietor died in 1936, the clinic was closed. Then in the late forties, local drugstore owner and real estate man Leon Adickes commissioned Raiford to design a new six-bed clinic, which was built in 1950 and expanded to a ten-bed facility in the late fifties, after Adickes sold it to Dr. Grover Winslow. But Dr. Winslow was not a surgeon, and for county residents to obtain comprehensive health care they had to travel to Nacogdoches, Houston, Beaumont, Lufkin, or Jasper. Finally, in the mid-seventies, Adickes spearheaded a drive to build a state-of-the-art hospital in Hemphill, commissioning Raiford to design a thirty-six-bed facility on the west side of town that has since become a model for rural county hospitals nationwide.

The project began in 1975 with the creation of the county's first hospital district and the election of a five-member board of

Entrance to Sabine County Hospital, Hemphill. (Photograph by Laura Cicarella)

directors. After passage of a bond issue in 1977 and receipt of a loan from the Farm and Home Administration (FmHA), the board called for a design that would put patient-care areas—operating and delivery rooms, labs, and nursing station—at the core of a 22,500-square-foot, one-story main building, surrounded by a corridor and patient rooms. Other patient-care as well as service areas—isolation room, intensive care unit, kitchen, cafeteria, and offices—were to be arranged around the building's perimeter, and an adjoining wing of patient rooms was to be designed to accommodate future expansion on the wooded, nine-acre site. The board also wanted a maintenance-free ex-

terior, one that would require little or no painting.

The hospital could have been built of concrete block and sufficiently served those purposes, but Raiford and Raggy talked the board into spending a little more money to clad it in a brownish gray brick veneer; spruce it up with white pilasters, lintels, corbeled brick, and other Greek Revival details; and top it all with a standing-seam metal roof, which is in the form of a sloping mansard except at the main entrance, where a hipped portion covers a columnar porch. Now, as Raiford says, "It has all the dignity that a building needs." (Raiford also remembers that one board member wanted to

Round windows, Sabine County Hospital, Hemphill. (Photograph by Laura Cicarella)

build the hospital of red brick, but Raiford was so determined to match the brick with the trunks of surrounding pine trees that he told him he had already ordered the brownish gray brick, when in fact he hadn't. "I didn't want to hurt his feelings," Raiford says.)

The main building, construction of which was begun in the fall of 1978 and completed in the spring of 1980, also includes a lobby, two emergency rooms, an emergency waiting room, six restrooms, patient-wing day room and waiting room, chapel, vending area, doctors' charting room, nurses' charting room, x-ray viewing room and darkroom, doctors' lounge and locker room, nurses' lounge and locker room, pharmacy, head nurse's office, storage and equipment areas, and janitors' rooms.

The structure of the building is steel frame on a concrete pier, beam, and slab foundation. Inside, metal wall studs are covered with gypsum board, with corridor walls finished in a vinyl wallcovering. Floors are vinyl-covered asbestos tile, and ceilings are suspended acoustical tile.

The hospital was expanded in 1982 with a two-level addition on the south side. Within the same Neo-Greek Revival exterior are a number of new or enlarged accommodations, including a nuclear medicine treatment room; pharmacy; ultrasound treatment room; physical-therapy area with whirlpool baths; respiratory-therapy room; storage rooms; and a new waiting room, which connects the addition to the main building. Raggy, who designed the new addition, is proud to point out that the $414,000 project was completely financed by operating funds from the hospital's first two years of service to Sabine County. (Dr. Winslow, meanwhile, has built a new doctor's office and outpatient clinic right next door, and Raiford and Raggy have been commissioned to design yet another addition to the hospital.)

From the beginning, support for the hospital was resounding. The bond issue passed two to one (due in part, perhaps, to the number of retirees in the county who live around the Toledo Bend Reservoir). The project also marked the first time in Texas that a complete hospital was funded by the FmHA, which normally lends money only to expand or buy equipment for an existing facility. In this case, the FmHA—part of the Department of Agriculture—helped pay for the design and construction of the entire main building and is absolutely delighted by the results, from the level of community enthusiasm for it to the quality of its design.

Owned and operated by the Sabine County Hospital District, the Sabine County Hospital is staffed by three full-time doctors, all of whom live in the county, some fifty other employees, is on the circuit of a dozen call-in physicians and dentists, and is open twenty-four hours a day, seven days a week, making Hemphill—with a population of fifteen hundred—something of a regional medical center for this farthest reach of Deep East Texas.

Other Restorations by Raiford Stripling

Completed

Beaty-Orton House, Jasper
Campbell Lott House, Goliad
Christ Episcopal Church, San Augustine
Columbus Cartwright House,
    San Augustine
Dallas Street Bar, Jefferson
French's Trading Post, Beaumont
Herring House, San Augustine
Horn-Polk House, San Augustine
Jack McKinney House, Chireno
Jewish Temple, Corsicana
Jim Alford House, Caldwell

Monroe-Crook House, Crockett
Old Jail, San Augustine
Quarters Eight, Fort Concho
Rex Payne Building, Center
Sandhop House, Palestine
San Jacinto County Jail, Coldspring
Sweeny Building, Houston
T. N. B. Greer House, San Augustine
Tiller House, San Augustine
W. I. Davis Building, Center
William Wade House, San Augustine

Planned

Alan McNeill House, Beaumont (consultant)
Buck Debney House, Jasper
Fanthorpe Inn, Anderson
General Store, Terlingua
Guinn House, Rusk
Halfway Inn, Chireno
James Gaines House, Sabine County
James Perkins House, Rusk
John Henry Kirby Birthplace, Chester
Judge Phillips House, Victoria

La Bahía Customs House, Goliad
Madam Garcia's House, Goliad
Madison Cooper House, Waco (consultant)
Manson-Hartman House, Rockwall
Old U.S. Arsenal, San Antonio (consultant)
Oliphant House, Sabine County
Pillot Building, Houston (consultant)
William George House, Richmond (consultant)

Notes on Sources

To avoid clogging the narrative with information that might be only marginally useful to non-academic readers, I have kept footnotes to a minimum, citing only those quoted and referenced passages I drew from other written works. I have presented all other quotations—whether communicated to me by personal interview, telephone, correspondence, or videotape—as though they were spoken, citing their sources in the body of the sentence.

This book, as do most, also includes a great many fragments of information from books, articles, pamphlets, reports, theses, dissertations, transcripts, and videotapes that were written and produced by other people. I will be forever in their debt. To measure the range of my research, the reader can refer to the bibliography, which I compiled as a comprehensive collection of sources as well as suggestions for further reading. (All the sources mentioned in the following chapter-by-chapter breakdown are cited in full in the bibliography.)

Also, as architects tend to be, Raiford is a man of images and not of words. Therefore, there is no extensive collection of letters or papers written by Raiford that would shed light on his life. I have, however, enjoyed access to a wealth of drawings, paintings, and photographs that reveal a good deal about his talents and sensibilities. I have also had the pleasure and privilege of talking at length with Raiford himself (a living subject may be a handicap to some biographers, but it was a great benefit to this one). While his insights proved invaluable, however, his memory was faulty at times, and some of the dates mentioned as matters of fact are only to the best of Raiford's recollection. In any case, I beg the indulgence of scholars who believe there is no such thing as too many footnotes, and I hope they will read this book with belief as well as enjoyment.

Chapter 1. Introduction: A Man and His Place

This look at aspects of Raiford and his habitat, as well as the regional and stylistic influences on his work, is drawn from my visits to San Augustine and its environs; from personal interviews, telephone conversations, and correspondence with Raiford, Raiford R. ("Raggy") Stripling, Frances Hartley, and Eugene George; and from the works of Drury Blakeley Alexander, George L. Crocket, Talbot Hamlin, William Dudley Hunt, Jr., Terry G. Jordan, Louis R. Nardini, Thomas R. Plaut and Mildred C. Anderson, John W. Reps, Joe C. Truett and Daniel W. Lay, Ernest Allen Connally, Elliot A. P. Evans, Richard West, Katy Capt, Amy Freeman Lee, and Victor Treat.

Other sources used in this chapter include the *Atlas of Texas*, by the Bureau of Business Research at the University of Texas at Austin; *San Augustine, "the Cradle of Texas,"* by the San Augustine County Development Association; *Pro-*

ceedings, Texana I: The Frontier, Round Top, 1980 and *Proceedings, Texana II: Cultural Heritage of the Plantation South, Jefferson,* both by the Texas Historical Commission; a computer printout of registered architects in Deep East Texas, provided by the Texas Board of Architectural Examiners; "San Augustine Comprehensive Plan," prepared by Brady Associates, Inc., of Fort Worth; *Poverty in Texas 1973* and *Texas Statistical Data Re-*

lated to Low-Income Persons by County, by the Office of Economic Opportunity, Texas Department of Community Affairs; *Community Data Profile—San Augustine,* by the Texas Industrial Commission; and the *1980 Census of Population,* vol. I, *Characteristics of the Population,* Chapter C, *General Social and Economic Characteristics,* Part 45, *Texas,* by the U.S. Department of Commerce, Bureau of the Census.

Chapter 2. Provenance

Genealogy of the Striplings and Leakes is derived in large part from research already done by Frances Hartley, Raiford's oldest sister, who provided me with copies of correspondence and excerpts from books, articles, and other documents having to do with their family history. These include works by George Warren Chappelear and Katy Capt; articles from the *San Augustine Tribune* and *Inland Architect and News Record;* the 1907 edition of Southwestern Univer-

sity's yearbook, the *Sou'wester;* an application for membership in the National Society of the Daughters of the American Colonists, prepared by Frances Hartley; and letters to Frances from Temple Phinney and Lance Swift.

The narrative was also compiled from personal interviews, telephone conversations, and correspondence with Frances Hartley, Raiford, Robert E. Stripling, Raiford R. Stripling, J. P. Mathews, and Kathleen Todd.

Chapter 3. Bayonets and Smocks

This account of the evolution of the Agricultural and Mechanical College of Texas and its architectural curriculum, and of Raiford's formative years there as a student and apprentice, came primarily from works by C. W. Crawford et al., Henry C. Dethloff, George Sessions Perry, Katy Capt, and Ernest Langford.

Other information was obtained from the 1926 to 1931 editions of the Texas A&M yearbook, *The Longhorn; Gold Book, Agricultural and Mechanical College of Texas: A Tribute to Her Loyal Sons Who*

Paid the Supreme Sacrifice in the World War, edited by N. M. McGinnis; and *Progress Report for Twelve Years of the Agricultural and Mechanical College of Texas 1925–1937.* Further information was obtained through my own visits to College Station and the A&M campus and from personal interviews, telephone conversations, and correspondence with Raiford, Bartlett Cocke, C. A. Johnson, J. P. Mathews, Jesse Leo Norton, Bonnie Sears, Robert E. Stripling, and Bradley Vosper.

Chapter 4. Prospects

My depiction of the historic preservation movement in the United States and Texas, Raiford's pioneering involvement in it, and of the historical significance of the Goliad missions is based mainly on information from the works of Carlos E. Castañeda, T. R. Fehrenbach, James Marston Fitch, Charles B. Hosmer, Jr., R. Furneaux Jordan, Walter F. McCaleb, Muriel Quest McCarthy, Carol McMichael, Rexford Newcomb, Hank Todd Smith, Daralice D. Boles, Hal Box, Stephen Fox, Larry Paul Fuller, Peter C. Papademetriou, Roy Eugene Graham, and Katy Capt.

Further information came from *Monuments Commemorating the Centenary of Texas Independence: The Report of the Commission of Control for Texas Centennial Celebrations; Historic Preservation in Texas,* vol. I, *The Comprehensive Statewide Historic Preservation Plan for Texas,* by the Texas Historical Commission; *Architectural Record;* and the La Villita historic district inventory nomination form for the National Register of Historic Places, prepared for the National Park Service. I also spoke at length with Raiford about historic architecture in Texas and its preservation in the 1930s.

Chapter 5. *Bird Dogs and La Bahía*

Raiford's life and its setting from World War II on—his camouflage work in Washington for the navy, his run-ins with a new breed of preservationist, his present San Augustine practice—are recounted here from personal interviews, telephone conversations, and correspondence with Raiford, Raiford R. Stripling, Robert E. Stripling, Frances Hartley, Roberta Garner, Dennis Cordes, David Hoffman, Binnie Hoffman, Peter Maxon, Peter Payne, Rawsie Payne, John Riley, Vincent Transano, and Bradley Vosper. I also obtained a good deal of information for this chapter from the works of Carlos E. Castañeda, James Marston Fitch, Guy Hartcup, Charles Jencks, Kathryn Stoner O'Connor, Konrad F. Wittmann, Paul Goldberger, Michael McCullar, R. Henderson Shuffler, and Katy Capt.

Other information was obtained from the *National Register of Historic Places in Texas*; *Texas Architect*; *Pampa Daily News*; and "Greek Revival Case Studies," a paper presented by Raiford at Winedale Workshop II.

Chapter 6. *Projects*

This look at Raiford's major projects, including the history of each structure (and excluding the Goliad restorations, which are described in chapters 4 and 5), is drawn largely from the works of the following authors: Drury Blakeley Alexander, Lavonia Jenkins Barnes, Howard Barnstone, Dorothy Kendall Bracken and Maurine Whorton Redway, Anne Clark, John S. Garner, Paul Goeldner, Virginia McAlester and Lee McAlester, Lester Walker, Marcus Whiffen, R. Henderson Shuffler, Tex Rogers, Dorothy Steinbomer Kendall, Phillipe Klinefelter, and Thomas M. Price.

I also obtained information for this chapter from a series of videotaped interviews of Raiford by Gordon Echols; *The Saccarappa* (newsletter of the Galveston Historical Society); docent training material prepared by the Historic Waco Foundation; inventory-nomination forms for the *National Register of Historic Places*; works edited by Beverly da Costa and Cyril M. Harris; and personal interviews, telephone conversations, and correspondence with Raiford, Raiford R. Stripling, Leon Adickes, Lavonia Jenkins Barnes, James Corbin, John Huntsinger, and Judy Schiebel.

Bibliography

Books

Alexander, Drury Blakeley. *Texas Homes of the 19th Century.* Austin: University of Texas Press, 1966.

Atlas of Texas. Austin: Bureau of Business Research, University of Texas at Austin, 1976.

Baer, Kurt. *Architecture of the California Missions.* Berkeley: University of California Press, 1958.

Barnes, Lavonia Jenkins. *Early Homes of Waco and the People Who Lived in Them.* Waco: Texian Press, 1970.

Barnstone, Howard. *The Galveston That Was.* Houston: Museum of Fine Arts, 1966.

Blake, Peter. *The Master Builders: Le Corbusier, Mies van der Rohe, Frank Lloyd Wright.* New York: W. W. Norton and Company, Inc., 1976.

Bracken, Dorothy Kendall, and Maurine Whorton Redway. *Early Texas Homes.* Dallas: Southern Methodist University Press, 1956.

Burchard, John, and Albert Bush-Brown. *The Architecture of America: A Social and Cultural History.* Boston: Little, Brown and Company, 1966.

Castañeda, Carlos E. *Our Catholic Heritage in Texas: 1519–1936.* 7 vols. Austin: Von Boeckmann-Jones, 1936–50.

Chappelear, George Warren. *Families of Virginia.* vol. I, *The Leake Family and Connecting Lines.* Dayton, Va.: Shenandoah Press, 1932.

Clark, Anne. *Historic Homes of San Augustine.* Austin: Encino Press, 1972.

Clark, Sarah. *The Capitols of Texas: A Visual History.* Austin: Encino Press, 1975.

Crawford, C. W., et al. *One Hundred Years of Engineering at Texas A&M 1876–1976.* N.p., 1976.

Crocket, George L. *Two Centuries in East Texas: A History of San Augustine County and Surrounding Territory from 1685.* San Augustine: Christ Episcopal Church, 1932.

Da Costa, Beverly, ed. *An American Heritage Guide: Historic Homes of America Open to the Public.* New York: American Heritage Publishing, 1971.

Dethloff, Henry C. *A Centennial History of Texas A&M University, 1876–1976.* 2 vols. College Station: Texas A&M University Press, 1975.

Fehrenbach, T. R. *Lone Star: A History of Texas and the Texans.* New York: American Legacy Press, 1978.

Fitch, James Marston. *Historic Preservation: Curatorial Management of the Built World.* New York: McGraw-Hill, 1982.

Garner, John S. *East Texas Architecture: A Select Study.* Austin: Texas Society of Architects, 1979.

Goeldner, Paul, comp. *Texas Catalog, Historic American Buildings Survey.* San Antonio: Trinity University Press, 1974.

Hamlin, Talbot. *Greek Revival Architecture in America: Being an Account of Important Trends in American Architecture and American Life Prior to the War between the States.* New York: Dover Publications, 1944.

Harris, Cyril M., ed. *Dictionary of Architecture and Construction.* New York: McGraw-Hill, 1975.

Hartcup, Guy. *Camouflage: A History of Conceal-*

ment and Deception in War. New York: Charles Scribner's Sons, 1980.

Henderson, Richard B. *Maury Maverick: A Political Biography.* Austin: University of Texas Press, 1970.

Hosmer, Charles B., Jr. *Presence of the Past: A History of the Preservation Movement in America before Williamsburg.* New York: G. P. Putnam's Sons, 1965.

———. *Preservation Comes of Age: From Williamsburg to the National Trust, 1926–1949.* 2 vols. Charlottesville: University Press of Virginia, 1981.

Hunt, William Dudley, Jr. *Encyclopedia of American Architecture.* New York: McGraw-Hill, 1980.

Jencks, Charles A. *The Language of Post-Modern Architecture.* New York: Rizzoli International Publications, 1977.

Jordan, R. Furneaux. *A Concise History of Western Architecture.* New York: Harcourt Brace Jovanovich, 1980.

Jordan, Terry G. *Texas Log Buildings: A Folk Architecture.* Austin: University of Texas Press, 1978.

Lane, J. J. *History of the University of Texas Based on Facts and Records.* Austin: Henry Hutchings State Printer, 1891.

Langford, Ernest. *The First Fifty Years of Architectural Education at the Agricultural and Mechanical College of Texas.* College Station: Texas A&M University Archives, 1957.

———. *Here We'll Build the College.* College Station: Texas A&M University Archives, 1963.

Lefever, Minard. *The Beauties of Modern Architecture.* New York: D. Appleton and Company, 1835.

The Longhorn (yearbook). College Station: Agricultural and Mechanical College of Texas, 1926–1931.

McAlester, Virginia, and Lee McAlester. *A Field Guide to American Houses.* New York: Alfred A. Knopf, 1984.

McCaleb, Walter F. *Spanish Missions of Texas.* San Antonio: The Naylor Company, 1954.

McCarthy, Muriel Quest. *David R. Williams, Pioneer Architect.* Dallas: Southern Methodist University Press, 1984.

McGinnis, N. M., ed. *Gold Gook, Agricultural & Mechanical College of Texas: A Tribute to Her Loyal Sons Who Paid the Supreme Sacrifice in*

the World War. College Station: Alumni Quarterly, August, 1919.

McMichael, Carol. Introduction to *Paul Cret at Texas: Architectural Drawings and the Image of the University in the 1930s,* by Drury Blakeley Alexander. Austin: Archer M. Huntington Art Gallery, College of Fine Arts, University of Texas at Austin, 1983.

Monuments Commemorating the Centenniary of Texas Independence: The Report of the Commission of Control for Texas Centennial Celebrations. Austin, 1938.

Nardini, Louis R. *No Man's Land: A History of El Camino Real.* New Orleans: Pelican Publishing, 1961.

Newcomb, Rexford. *Spanish Colonial Architecture in the United States.* New York: S. J. Augustin, 1937.

Nicholson, Arnold. *American Houses in History.* New York: Viking Press, 1965.

O'Connor, Kathryn Stoner. *The Presidio La Bahía del Espíritu Santo de Zuñiga, 1721 to 1846.* Austin: Von Boeckmann-Jones, 1966.

Pass, Fred, ed. *Texas Almanac and State Industrial Guide 1980–1981.* 50th ed. Dallas: A. H. Belo, 1979.

Perry, George Sessions. *The Story of Texas A&M.* New York: McGraw-Hill, 1951.

Plaut, Thomas R., and Mildred C. Anderson. *Gross Regional Product of Texas and Its Regions.* Austin: Bureau of Business Research, University of Texas at Austin, 1981.

Progress Report for Twelve Years of the Agricultural and Mechanical College of Texas 1925–1937. College Station, n.d.

Reps, John W. *The Forgotten Frontier: Urban Planning in the American West before 1890.* Columbia: University of Missouri Press, 1981.

Robinson, Willard B. *Gone from Texas: Our Lost Architectural Heritage.* College Station: Texas A&M University Press, 1981.

San Augustine County Development Association. *San Augustine, "the Cradle of Texas."* Diboll: The Free Press, n.d.

San Augustine, "the Cradle of Texas": 23rd Annual Tour, Medallion Homes and Historical Places. San Augustine: Ezekiel Cullen Chapter, Daughters of the Republic of Texas, 1983.

Shurtleff, Harold R. *The Log Cabin Myth: A Study of the Early Dwellings of the English Colonists in North America.* Edited by Samuel Eliot

Morison. Cambridge: Harvard University Press, 1939.

Sitwell, Sacheverell. *Baroque and Rococo.* New York: G. P. Putnam's Sons, 1967.

Smith, Hank Todd. *Since 1886: A History of the Texas Society of Architects.* Austin: Texas Society of Architects, 1983.

Sou'wester (yearbook). Georgetown, Tex.: Southwestern University, 1907.

Stripling, Robert E. *The Red Plot against America.* Edited by Bob Considine. Drexel Hill, Pa.: Bell Publishing, 1949.

Texas Historical Commission. *Historic Preservation in Texas.* vol. I, *The Comprehensive Statewide Historic Preservation Plan for Texas.* Austin, 1973.

———. *Proceedings, Texana I: The Frontier, Round Top, 1980.* Austin, 1983.

———. *Proceedings, Texana II: Cultural Heritage of the Plantation South, Jefferson, 1981.* Austin, 1982.

———. *Texas Preservation Handbook for County Historical Commissions.* Austin, 1984.

———. *The National Register of Historic Places in Texas.* Austin, 1979.

Tinkle, Lon, Joe Schmitz, Dorman Winfrey, Joe B. Frantz, James M. Day, and Ben Proctor. *Six Missions of Texas.* Waco: Texian Press, 1965.

Truett, Joe C., and Daniel W. Lay. *Land of Bears and Honey: A Natural History of East Texas.* Austin: University of Texas Press, 1984.

Venturi, Robert. *Complexity and Contradiction in Architecture.* New York: Museum of Modern Art, 1966.

Vines, Robert A. *Trees of East Texas.* Austin: University of Texas Press, 1977.

Walker, Lester. Preface to *American Shelter: An Illustrated Encyclopedia of the American House,* by Charles Moore, Woodstock, N.Y.: The Overlook Press, 1981.

Webb, Walter P., H. B. Carroll, and Stephen Eldon Branda, eds. *The Handbook of Texas.* 3 vols. Austin: Texas State Historical Association, 1952, 1976.

Welch, June Rayfield. *Historic Sites of Texas.* Dallas: G. L. A. Press, 1972.

Whiffen, Marcus. *American Architecture since 1780: A Guide to the Styles.* Cambridge: MIT Press, 1969.

Wittmann, Konrad F. *Industrial Camouflage Manual: Prepared for the Industrial Camouflage Program at Pratt Institute, Brooklyn, New York.* New York: Reinhold Publishing, 1942.

Zunker, Vernon G. *A Dream Come True: Robert Hugman and San Antonio's River Walk.* San Antonio: Vernon G. Zunker, 1983.

ARTICLES

Ayres, Atlee B. "The Earliest Mission Buildings of San Antonio, Texas." *American Architect—The Architectural Review* 126 (August 27, 1924): 171–78.

Boles, Daralice D. "Rethinking Ruskin." *Progressive Architecture* (November, 1984): 87.

Bostic, Elaine. "La Bahía: The Forgotten Fortress." *Texas Highways* (March, 1968): 8–13.

Box, Hal. "Texas Traditions: A Sense of Texas Architecture." *Architectural Review* 164 (November, 1978): 266–74.

Celoria, Miguel. "Spanish Colonial Architecture: An Archaeological Approach." *Journal of the Society of Architectural Historians* 34 (December, 1975): 295.

Connally, Ernest Allen. "Architecture at the End of the South: Central Texas." *Journal of the Society of Architectural Historians* 2 (December, 1952): 8–12.

Echols, Gordon. "Profile: Raiford Stripling, the Dean of Restoration Architects in Texas." *Texas Architect* 32 (January-February, 1982): 38–39.

Evans, Elliot A. P. "The East Texas House." *Journal of the Society of Architectural Historians* 2 (December, 1952): 1–6.

Fox, Stephen. "Tall Tales from the Borderland: Brownsville and the Spanish Colonial Revival." *Texas Architect* 31 (July-August, 1981): 59–65.

Fuller, Larry Paul. "Interview: O'Neil Ford." *Texas Architect* 28 (May-June, 1978).

Goldberger, Paul. "Preserving the Original Function as Well as Detail Is Key to Today's Restoration." *New York Times Magazine*, October 7, 1984.

"Holabird and Roche, Architects." *Inland Architect and News Record* 51 (March, 1908).

Laurence, F. S. "The Old Spanish Missions in and about San Antonio." *American Architect—The Architectural Review* 124 (November 21, 1923): 445–50.

Leslie, Candace. "Raiford Stripling: Man with a

Mission." *Texas Homes* 7 (May, 1983): 25–31.

Malsch, Brownson. "Famous Goliad Landmarks 250 Years Old." *Texas Star*, December 17, 1972.

McCullar, Michael. "Profile: Bell, Klein, and Hoffman, Austin Architects and Restoration Consultants, Inc." *Texas Architect* 32 (January-February, 1982): 32–36.

———. "Raiford Stripling Honored at San Antonio Symposium." *Texas Architect* 33 (November-December, 1983).

Moore, Roger, and Texas Anderson. "Gilded Age Archaeology: The Ashton Villa." *Archaeology* (May-June, 1984): 44–50.

Nelson, George. "Mission Architecture." *Arts and Decoration* 45 (October, 1936).

Newcomb, Rexford. "A Remnant of Spanish Renaissance Architecture in Texas." *Western Architect* 28 (January, 1919): 3–5.

Papademetriou, Peter C. "Nationalism-Regionalism, Modernism: In Search of a Texas Architecture." *Texas Architect* 28 (May-June, 1978): 17–21.

———. "Texas Regionalism 1925–1950: An Elusive Sensibility." *Texas Architect* 31 (July-August, 1981): 36–41.

"Remembering Goliad." *Houston Post Spotlight* December 11, 1966, p. 14.

"The Restoration of Colonial Williamsburg in Virginia." *Architectural Record* 78 (December, 1935).

Selden, Jack. "Remember Goliad!" *Texas Highways* (October, 1984): 24–29.

Shuffler, R. Henderson. "The Signing of Texas' Declaration of Independence: Myth and Record." *Southwestern Historical Quarterly* 65 (July, 1961–April, 1962): 310–332.

Swank, A. B. "The Villita Project." *Southwest Review* 25 (July, 1940): 394–403.

Walters, Jonathan. "Main Street Turns the Corner." *Historic Preservation* (November-December, 1981): 37–45.

West, Richard. "The Petrified Forest." *Texas Monthly* 6 (April, 1978).

"What Price Preservation: Financial Incentives for Saving Old Buildings." *Texas Architect* 32 (January-February, 1982): 60–61.

Williams, David R. "Toward a Southwestern Architecture." *Southwest Review* 16 (April, 1931): 301–313.

NEWSPAPERS

Austin American-Statesman, May 12, 1946; June 2, 1955; October 6, 1957; February 12, 1958.

Dallas Morning News, April, 29, 1983.

Houston Post, May 2, 1968; July 6, 1969.

New York Times, July 9, 1984.

Pampa Daily News, February 11, 1958.

San Augustine Tribune, February 23, 1969.

The Saccarappa [Galveston Historical Society], June-July, 1974.

UNPUBLISHED MATERIAL

Application for Membership in National Society, Daughters of the American Colonists. Prepared by Mrs. Frances Stripling Hartley. N.p., June 26, 1982.

Capt, Katy. "Raiford Leak Stripling: The Life and Times of an East Texas Restoration Architect." Master's thesis, Texas A&M University, 1981.

Connally, Ernest Allen. "The Ecclesiastical and Military Architecture of the Spanish Province of Texas." Ph.D. dissertation, Harvard University, 1955.

Graham, Roy Eugene. "Progressive Preservation: A Guide to the Understanding and Implementation of the Preservation of Historical Architecture in Texas." University of Texas at Austin, 1972.

Historic Waco Foundation. "Earle-Napier-Kinnard House," docent training material. Waco, n.d.

———. "East Terrace," docent training material. Waco, n.d.

———. "Fort House Museum," docent training material. Waco, n.d.

"Hotels Designed by Holabird and Roche." Notebook in the library of the Chicago Art Institute (ca. 1915), pp. 4–18.

Kendall, Dorothy Steinbomer. "French Influence on the Architecture of Texas." N.p., n.d.

Klinefelter, Phillipe. "Critical Essay on the French Legation." University of Texas at Austin, 1981.

Lee, Amy Freeman. Introductory remarks, program no. 2, "Texas, a Sense of Place, a Spirit of Independence: Raiford Stripling, Dean of Historic Restoration in Texas." Script for videotape recording produced by Dick Rizzo with the participation of Victor Treat,

Gordon Echols, and José Miguel Fernandez. College Station: KAMU-TV, 1983.

Price, Thomas. M. "Architecture in Galveston." Lecture presented as part of Ashton Villa Docent Committee lecture series, Galveston, April 17, 1974.

"San Augustine Comprehensive Plan." Fort Worth: Brady and Associates, n.d.

Stripling, Raiford. "Greek Revival Case Studies." Paper presented at Winedale Workshop II: A Conference on the Principles of Architectural Preservation and Restoration, Texas University Winedale Inn Properties, September 12–13, 1969.

———. "Walking Tour of Ashton Villa with Mr. Stripling." Transcript of interview by members of the Galveston Historical Foundation. Galveston, 1974.

Texas Board of Architectural Examiners. Registered architects in Deep East Texas. Computer printout. Austin, August, 1974.

Treat, Victor. "Raiford Leak Stripling: Restoration Architect." Paper presented at the annual meeting of the Texas State Historical Association, Austin, March, 1984.

PUBLIC DOCUMENTS

Minutes of Commissioners Court Record, vol. G, August 8, 1927. San Augustine County, 1924–1933.

Texas Department of Community Affairs. Office of Economic Opportunity. *Poverty in Texas 1973*. Austin, 1974.

———. *Texas Statistical Data Related to Low-Income Persons by County*. Austin, September 25, 1981.

Texas Industrial Commission. Research and Data Services Department. *Community Data Profile—San Augustine*. Austin, September, 20, 1983.

U.S. Department of Commerce. Bureau of the Census. *1980 Census of Population*, vol. I, *Characteristics of the Population, Chapter C, General Social and Economic Characteristics, Part 45, Texas*. Washington, D.C., July, 1983.

U.S. Department of the Interior. National Park Service. *National Register of Historic Places Inventory-Nomination Form, Ashton Villa*. Prepared by Wayne Bell, Texas State Histor-

ical Survey Committee. Austin, August 18, 1969.

———. *National Register of Historic Places Inventory-Nomination Form, Earle-Napier-Kinnard House*. Prepared by Wayne Bell and Roxanne Williamson, Texas State Historical Survey Committee. Austin, November 5, 1970.

———. *National Register of Historic Places Inventory-Nomination Form, Ezekiel Cullen House*. Prepared by Wayne Bell and Gary Hume, Texas State Historical Survey Committee. Austin, March 17, 1971.

———. *National Register of Historic Places Inventory-Nomination Form, Fort House*. Prepared by Wayne Bell and Roxanne Williamson, Texas State Historical Survey Committee. Austin, July 20, 1970.

———. *National Register of Historic Places Inventory-Nomination Form, Fort House*. Prepared by Wayne Bell and Roxanne Williamson, Texas State Historical Survey Committee. Austin, July 20, 1970.

———. *National Register of Historic Places Inventory-Nomination Form, John Wesley Mann House*. Prepared by Wayne Bell and Roxanne Williamson, Texas State Historical Survey Committee. Austin, May 6, 1971.

———. *National Register of Historic Places Inventory-Nomination Form, La Villita Historic District*. Prepared by Wayne Bell, Gary Hume, and Roxanne Williamson, Texas State Historical Survey Committee. Austin, November 18, 1971.

———. *National Register of Historic Places Inventory-Nomination Form, Matthew Cartwright House*. Prepared by Wayne Bell, Gary Hume, and Roxanne Williamson, Texas State Historical Survey Committee. Austin, September 28, 1970.

PERSONAL COMMUNICATION

Adickes, Leon. Telephone conversation with author, November 20, 1984.

Barnes, Lavonia Jenkins. Telephone conversation with author, November 15, 1984.

Cocke, Bartlett. Telephone conversation with author, August 13, 1984.

Corbin, James. Telephone conversation with author, September 25, 1984.

Cordes, Dennis. Telephone conversation with author, July 31, 1984.

———. Telephone conversation with author, September 26, 1984.

Garner, Roberta. Letter to author, July 14, 1984.

———. Telephone conversation with author, July 18, 1984.

George, Eugene. Telephone conversation with author, n.d. [fall of 1983].

Hartley, Frances. Letter to author, March 20, 1984.

Hoffman, David. Interview with author. Austin, Texas, August 6, 1984.

Hoffman, Binnie. Interview with author. Austin, Texas, August 6, 1984.

Huntsinger, John. Telephone conversation with author, November 26, 1984.

Johnson, C. A. Letter to author, May 28, 1984.

Lasell, Inez. Telephone conversation with author, November 15, 1984.

Mathews, J. P. Letter to author, April 12, 1984.

Maxon, Peter. Telephone conversation with author, n.d. [spring of 1984].

Miller, J. D. Telephone conversation with author, November 21, 1984.

Norton, Jesse Leo. Letter to author, March 13, 1984.

Payne, Peter. Interview with author. San Augustine, Texas, December 5–10, 1983.

Payne, Rawsie. Interview with author. San Augustine, Texas, December 5–10, 1983.

Phinney, Temple. Letter to Frances Hartley, March 14, 1984.

Riley, John. Telephone conversation with author, September 19, 1984.

Sears, Bonnie A. Letter to author, August 27, 1984.

Schiebel, Judy. Telephone conversation with author, n.d. [summer of 1984].

Stripling, Raiford L. Letter to Frances Stripling, September 12, 1937.

———. Interview with author. San Augustine, Texas, December 5–10, 1983.

———. Interview with author. San Augustine, Texas, September 6, 1984.

———. Interview by Gordon Echols, n.d. Videotape recordings, College of Architecture and Environmental Design, Texas A&M University, College Station.

Stripling, Raiford R. Interview with author. San Augustine, Texas, December 5–10, 1983.

———. Letter to author, n.d. [September, 1984].

Stripling, Robert E. Letter to author, March 1, 1984.

———. Letter to author, March 5, 1984.

Swift, Lance. Letter to Winfrey Leak Stripling and Mary Jane Stripling, November 5, 1975.

Todd, Kathleen. Letter to author, May 2, 1984.

Vosper, Bradley. Telephone conversation with author, April 5, 1985.

Index

(Page numbers in bold face type refer to illustration captions.)

Public Works Administration. *See* PWA
PWA, 46, 47

Ragland, Roberta, 61. *See also* Stripling,
    Roberta Ragland; Garner, Roberta
Ramsdell, Charles, 53, 54
Ramsey, Ben, 5
rectified photography, 93
Refugio, 49
Regulator-Moderator War, 5
RepublicBank, Houston, 101
Rice Institute, Houston, 24
"River House." *See* East Terrace
River Walk, San Antonio. *See* Paseo del
    Rio
Roberts, Benjamin, 127
Roberts, Elisha, 127
Roberts, King, 20, 21
Roberts, O. M., 5
Robertson, Joseph W., 131, 132, 133
Rockefeller, John D., Jr., 42
Roosevelt, Eleanor, 13, 57
Roosevelt, Franklin D., 44
ROTC, 28, 30–32
Ruffini, Frederick E., 46
Rusk, Thomas J., 50
Ruskin, John, 42

Saarinen, Eero, 100
Sabine County Hospital, Hemphill, 98,
    141, **142**, 140–43
Sabine County Hospital District, 143
Sam Houston State University, Hunts-
    ville, 96
San Antonio, 44; preservation efforts
    in, 70
San Antonio Conservation Society, 58,
    70
San Augustine: architecture of, 5, 12;
    character of, 4; description of, 4; his-
    tory of, 4–5, 17; life in, 19, 66; loca-
    tion of, 4; restoration projects in,
    116–28
San Augustine County Courthouse, 24,
    35
San Augustine County Historical
    Society, 69
San Augustine County Jail. *See* Old Jail,
    San Augustine
San Augustine University, 5, 124
San José. *See* Mission San José y San
    Miguel de Aguayo
Santa Anna, Antonio López de, 49, 50
sawmills, 12, 12 n.5
Schiebel, Judy, 137
Schuchard, Ernst, 97
Scottish Rite Cathedral, San Antonio,
    33
Scurlock House, 101
Sessums, Charles M., 28
Shriners' Temple, Dallas, 33

Shuffler, R. Henderson, 95, 139
Simons, Shirley, 24, 25, 35, 37, 97
Sloan, John E., 32
Smith, Harvey P., 58, 94
Smith, Robert, 101
social life, 25, 39, 61, 67–68. *See also*
    hunting
Sons of the Republic of Texas, 6
Spanish Governor's Palace, San An-
    tonio, 95
Spanish missions. *See* missions
Stephen W. Blount House. *See* Blount
    House
stereophotogrammetry, 93
Stripling, Abner (great-grandfather), 15
Stripling, Benjamin (grandfather), 15,
    16, 21
Stripling, Bob (great-uncle), 15, 16
Stripling, Essie (wife of Robert), 64, 67
Stripling, Frances ("Fannie") (great-
    aunt), 15, 16
Stripling, Frances (sister), 14, 18, 19,
    37, 60–61
Stripling, Jake (uncle), 16
Stripling, John (uncle), 16
Stripling, Mack (cousin), 16
Stripling, Martha (sister), 19, 67
Stripling, Mary Jane (sister), 19, 99
Stripling, Missouri ("Zoo") Axley
    (great-aunt), 15
Stripling, Narcissa Johnson (grand-
    mother), 15, 16
Stripling, Raiford ("Raif") Nichols (fa-
    ther): career, 17, 18; character, 17, 20,
    22, 26, 41; early life, 15–18; photo-
    graph, **19**. *See also* Stripling & Bur-
    rows; Stripling's Drugstore
Stripling, Raiford Ragland ("Raggy")
    (son): early life, 65, 66; partnership
    with father, 5, 97–98, 141, 143; pho-
    tograph, **65**; relationship with father,
    67, 98, 99; reminiscences about fa-
    ther, 66, 71, 98, 100
Stripling, Robert (brother): early life,
    19, 24, 35; employment as congres-
    sional aide, 35–36, 64; photograph,
    19; reminiscences about father, 18,
    42; reminiscences about Raiford,
    20–21, 25, 67, 100
Stripling, Roberta Ragland (wife), 61,
    65, 65, 66. *See also* Garner, Roberta
Stripling, Sam (uncle), 15, 16, 17
Stripling, Sarah (sister), 19, 100
Stripling, Winfrey Robbie Leak
    (mother), 18, 19, 21, 22, 24
"Stripling": origin of name, 9
Stripling and Burrows, 17, 18
Stripling family, 15
Stripling-Hazelwood Drug Company,
    17
Stripling's Drugstore, 8, 18, 20, 66, 99

Sullivan, Louis, 23–24
symposium, 11, 14

Tax Reform Act of 1976, 96
technology. *See* preservation tech-
    nology
Texaco, 36
Texas Agricultural and Mechanical Col-
    lege (Texas A&M): academic program
    at, 28; Administration Building at, 38;
    architecture department at, 28–32;
    architecture department at, Beaux
    Arts training in, 6, 32; building cam-
    paign at, 37, 38; description of, 27,
    28; effect of depression on, 39; enroll-
    ment figures for, 27–28; founding
    and purpose of, 26; funding of, 27,
    37; hazing at, 28; legislation for uni-
    versity system at, 27; life at, 30–32;
    military regimen at, 28; office of the
    college architect at, 34, 37–38; School
    of Engineering at, 28; University of
    Texas relationship to, 27; vocational
    programs at, 26
Texas Centennial, 65
Texas Centennial Advisory Board of
    Texas Historians, 47
Texas Centennial Commission of Con-
    trol, 47, 58
Texas Centennial Exposition, 47
Texas Historical Commission (THC), 89,
    94, 95, 96
Texas Parks and Wildlife Department,
    89, 92, 93, 140
Texas Revolution, 48–50, 138–39
Texas State Association of Architects,
    57
Texas State Building Commission, 94
Texas state capitol, 46
Texas State Historical Survey Commit-
    tee, 69, 89. *See also* Texas Historical
    Commission
Thornton, William, 6
Tiro al Pichon Association, 101
Transco Tower, Houston, 101
Travis, William B., 49
Turner, Johnathan B., 26

Udall, Stuart, 87–88
United States Capitol, 6
United States Centennial Commission,
    47
University Baptist Church, Austin, 46
University of Texas: architecture depart-
    ment of, 33; buildings at, 40, 45, 46;
    founding of, 27; funding of, 37, 40;
    office of the supervising architect at,
    45. *See also* Permanent University
    Fund
University of Virginia, Charlottesville,
    6, 12